GOOD EATING
BARBECUE

GOOD EATING

BARBECUE

YOUR COMPLETE GUIDE TO CREATING PERFECT BARBECUES EVERY TIME

This edition published in 2012

LOVE FOOD is an imprint of Parragon Books Ltd

Parragon
Queen Street House
4 Queen Street
Bath BA1 1HE, UK

ISBN 978-1-4454-6609-5

Printed in China

Cover design by Talking Design

Notes for the Reader

This book uses both imperial and metric measurements. Follow the same units of measurement
throughout; do not mix imperial and metric. All spoon measurements are level: teaspoons are assumed to
be 5 ml, and tablespoons are assumed to be 15 ml. Unless otherwise stated, milk is assumed to be full fat,
eggs and individual vegetables are medium, and pepper is freshly ground black pepper.

The times given are an approximate guide only. Preparation times differ according to the techniques used
by different people and the cooking times may also vary from those given as a result of the type of oven
used. Optional ingredients, variations, or serving suggestions have not been included in the calculations.

Recipes using raw or very lightly cooked eggs should be avoided by infants, the elderly, pregnant women,
convalescents, and anyone with a chronic condition. Pregnant and breast-feeding women are advised to
avoid eating peanuts and peanut products. People with nut allergies should be aware that some of the
prepared ingredients used in the recipes in this book may contain nuts. Always check the package before
use.

CONTENTS

INTRODUCTION

Barbecuing is not only a delicious way to cook food outdoors, it is also lots of fun. Whether you are cooking a small weekend lunch for the family or throwing a party for a number of guests, a barbecue can provide plenty of variety and entertainment for everyone. A barbecue party can be one of the easiest, most sociable and flexible ways to entertain – it can start in the afternoon and stretch lazily into the evening, with guests arriving and leaving as they please. Barbecues need not be limited to the garden or patio either – you can easily take a portable or disposable barbecue along on a camping trip, a picnic on the beach or even a walk up a mountain! With a little forward planning you can cook a feast wherever you choose.

Although meat is the traditional barbecue staple, virtually any type of food can be cooked on a barbecue – from meat and poultry to seafood and vegetables, even desserts. If you're new to cooking on the barbecue, start by cooking simple dishes, such as burgers and steaks, until you build your confidence and become familiar with your barbecue. When you are ready to try something more complicated, you can experiment with a range of techniques, such as making kebabs on skewers, cooking foods in foil parcels and using marinades and rubs.

The Big Book of BBQ contains all the recipes you need to make the most of your barbecue, including some familiar classics and lots of new ideas too. You'll find recipes for a huge variety of barbecue favourites – including brilliant burgers, sizzling skewers, finger-licking spare ribs, fabulous fish and seafood, vegetarian feasts, scrumptious salads and side dishes, and delicious desserts and drinks. All the recipes include easy-to-follow instructions, so you can rely on them for good results every time. Each recipe is illustrated with a beautiful full-colour photograph to whet your appetite and inspire you to get cooking outdoors. If you're just a beginner, you'll find that the comprehensive introduction is packed with invaluable information to get you started, not to mention some useful tips to help you along the way. So what are you waiting for? Fire up the barbecue and get grilling!

GETTING STARTED

BASIC BARBECUING IN 10 EASY STEPS

1.Choose your type of barbecue

Disposable: This is the most inexpensive type of barbecue, perfect for a picnic or camping trip. It consists of a small foil tray containing charcoal and a metal rack over the top. It will last up to an hour and can only be used once.

Portable: As the name suggests, portable barbecues are easy to carry and can be folded away to fit into the boot of a car.

Brazier: One of the simplest designs and most inexpensive types of charcoal grills, this consists of a grill rack placed over a metal pan. Some have legs while others have wheels, but they generally do not have a lid or venting system.

Kettle-grill: This is a popular type of barbecue – it is versatile and efficient and can be used with the lid on for smoking and roasting foods. The lid also offers protection from the wind and rain. The temperature can easily be controlled using the air vents.

Permanent: A fixed barbecue is inexpensive to build in your garden and can be made of simple materials, such as bricks, a metal tray and a grill rack. It is an excellent choice if you cook outdoors frequently.

Gas: There is a huge variety of gas models on the market and the choice is really down to the size of your budget. They are incredibly simple to use but won't give food the smoky flavour traditionally associated with barbecuing.

2. Choose your fuel

Charcoal: Lumpwood charcoal is easy to ignite and inexpensive, but burns relatively quickly. Charcoal briquettes can take a while to ignite, but will burn for a long time with little smoke. Self-lighting charcoal is lumpwood charcoal or briquettes that have been coated with a flammable chemical. Ensure that you wait until the chemical has burnt off before cooking or it may taint the food.

Wood: This is trickier to use than charcoal because wood burns fiercely for a shorter time and then cools rapidly. Always use hardwoods, such as oak, apple or cherry, because they burn slower than softwoods and have a pleasant smell.

Gas: Various sizes of bottles and cylinders of propane or butane gas can be ordered from gas suppliers and delivered to your home, or bought from large hardware shops. Check the manufacturer's instructions for the correct type for your barbecue.

3. Get your tools ready

You will need long-handled tongs and spatulas for turning food and removing it once it is cooked. A brush is useful for brushing the food with oil or marinades during the cooking. Oven gloves are essential for preventing burnt hands. Keep a water spray handy for dealing with flare ups.

4. Pick your spot

If you are not using a fixed grill, be sure to choose a spot on a flat surface in an area that is sheltered from the wind. Keep the barbecue away from trees and shrubs. Once it is lit, do not move it.

5. Prepare the barbecue

If you are using a charcoal barbecue, use foil to line the base. This will make cleaning easier and keep the base of the barbecue hot. Spread a layer of fuel on the bottom of the barbecue – small pieces at the bottom and medium-sized pieces on top of them works best. The layer of charcoal or wood should be 5 cm/2 inches deep and resemble a pyramid in the centre of the grate (if you are using firelighters, see below).

Gas grills require no preparation, although it is advisable to check that you have plenty of gas left in the cylinder before you start cooking.

6. Light the barbecue

If using firelighter cubes, place one or two in the centre of the pyramid. If using liquid firelighter, pour a few tablespoons over the fuel. Light the barbecue using a long match or taper. If you are using a charcoal barbecue, remember that you will need to light it at least 40 minutes before you want to cook.

If using a gas barbecue, open the lid and then open the gas tank. Give the gas chamber

2 or 3 seconds to fill, then press the ignite button. Once all the burners are lit, close the lid to let it preheat. For further information, check the manufacturer's instructions.

7. Prepare to cook

When the charcoal is hot (about 30 minutes after lighting, depending on the type of charcoal used), it will glow a red to orange colour, then gradually turn a whitish grey. It is now ready to be spread over the base of the barbecue in an even layer.

Gas barbecues generally only take 10 minutes to heat up.

8. Control the heat

To control the heat of a charcoal grill for cooking, you can raise or lower the grill rack. If your barbecue has vents, open these to raise the temperature and close them to lower it.

The heat of a gas barbecue can be controlled at the flick of a switch. It's usually best to light the barbecue to its highest setting and reduce the heat as needed.

9. Get the food ready

If food has been chilled, return it to room temperature before cooking. Any frozen food should be completely defrosted. If any food has been marinated in a liquid, drain it thoroughly.

10. Get cooking

Do not overcrowd food on the grill rack because this will prevent it from cooking properly. You may want to use a separate grill for cooking vegetarian foods and desserts. Make sure to turn food frequently during cooking and check it is cooked all the way through before eating.

HINTS & TIPS

- Before you start cooking, ensure that the barbecue is very hot and that the grill rack is at the correct height. An easy way to gauge the heat is to hold out your hand above the grill rack. If you can keep it there for only 2–3 seconds, the barbecue is hot enough to sear meat – any longer and it is not hot enough.

- Hinged wire grill baskets are useful for cooking smaller items, which would otherwise fall through the grill rack. They also enable you to turn a whole fish without the risk of it breaking up.

- Try to resist the temptation to prod at steaks and burgers while they are cooking because this will cause the juices to drain away, making the meat dry.

- Use a wire brush to remove burnt-on food and debris from the grill rack between batches and to give it a final scrub when you have finished cooking. It is easier to clean the grill rack while it is still warm.

- For an easy way to oil the grill rack while cooking, soak a wad of kitchen paper in oil, grasp with long-handled tongs and rub firmly over the rack.

- Wooden skewers should be soaked in cold water for 30 minutes before using to prevent them from burning.

SAFETY

Fire safety

- Place the barbecue on level ground where it cannot wobble or tip over.
- Position the barbecue away from houses, sheds, fences and overhanging trees. A sheltered position will cut down the amount of smoke and embers blowing about.
- Keep pets and small children away from the barbecue to avoid accidents.
- Do not use any flammable liquids, other than purpose-made liquid firelighter, to try to speed up the ignition of the barbecue. Never use lighter fluid, petrol or alcohol.
- Have a bucket of water ready in case the fire gets out of control.
- Never leave a lit barbecue unattended.
- When you have finished cooking, push the coals away from the centre to speed up cooling. Remember that embers may still be hot even if they look like they've gone out. The cooled ash can be disposed of by turning it onto bare garden soil or into a plastic bag and then into the dustbin.
- Always store gas cylinders or bottles outside and protect them from direct sunlight and frost. It is not advisable to keep more spare cylinders than you need. Make sure to shut off the gas valves once you have finished cooking.

Food safety

- Store uncooked meat, poultry and fish in separate airtight containers in the refrigerator until 30 minutes before cooking. If there isn't enough space in the refrigerator, invest in a cool box with ice packs so you can store the food outside.

- Always wash your hands thoroughly after handling raw meat, poultry or fish.
- Use one set of tools to transfer raw foods to the barbecue, and another set for handling cooked food. Do not put raw and nearly-cooked food next to each other on the grill.
- To avoid food poisoning, always make sure that meat – in particular chicken, turkey and sausages – is cooked through. The cooked meat should have no pink flesh and the juices should run clear (not pink) when a skewer is inserted into the thickest part of the meat. You can buy special thermometers to test the internal temperature of larger pieces of meat, poultry or fish.
- If the marinade you are using for basting has been in contact with uncooked meat, poultry, fish or seafood, do not use it during the last few minutes of cooking otherwise any harmful bacteria may not be destroyed by the heat of the barbecue. The safest way is to reserve a portion of the marinade for basting before adding raw foods.

MARINADES

A marinade is a liquid or paste that is used to soak food before cooking. It helps to tenderize meat, poultry, fish and seafood, and adds flavour and moisture, ensuring that the food remains succulent throughout cooking.

Always marinate food in a non-metallic dish or in a plastic food bag. Food should be submerged in the marinade and turned from time to time. Resist the temptation to marinate for longer than stated as the food may become too soft. As a general rule, fish needs to be marinated for 2–3 hours, while meat can be marinated for up to 24 hours, depending on the actual marinade.

Sticky Barbecue Marinade

Especially good with pork spare ribs, sausages or chicken, this tasty marinade cooks to a gloriously sticky, flavoursome coating. Try using other types of preserves, such as apricot jam, redcurrant jelly or marmalade, in place of the plum jam.

Makes enough for about 500 g/1 lb 2 oz meat, poultry or fish
55 g/2 oz soft light or dark brown sugar
5 tbsp plum jam
2 tbsp tomato purée
2 tbsp white wine vinegar
1 tbsp wholegrain mustard

Heat all the ingredients in a saucepan over a low heat, stirring until smooth. Remove from the heat and leave to cool.

Meanwhile, score the meat, poultry or fish portions deeply with a sharp knife. Put the prepared meat, poultry or fish in a shallow non-metallic dish or plastic food bag.

Pour the marinade over the prepared meat, poultry or fish and turn to coat.

Cover tightly or seal and leave to marinate in the refrigerator, turning occasionally, for at least an hour or preferably, for meat only, overnight before cooking.

Tandoori Yogurt Marinade

This is a classic creamy Indian marinade, and provides just a hint of heat from the spices. It is an excellent marinade to enhance the flavours of a grilled rack of lamb or a chicken dish.

Makes enough for about 500 g/1 lb 2 oz meat, poultry or fish

1 tsp chilli powder
1 tsp ground turmeric
1 tsp ground cumin
1 tsp garam masala
1 tsp ground cinnamon
4 onions, finely chopped
2 garlic cloves, crushed
300 ml/10 fl oz natural yogurt
juice of 2 lemons
5 tbsp sunflower or groundnut oil
5 tbsp tomato purée
2 tbsp white or red wine vinegar
2 tbsp soft dark brown sugar

2 tsp grated fresh ginger
salt and pepper

Score the meat, poultry or fish portions deeply with a sharp knife. Put the prepared meat, poultry or fish in a shallow non-metallic dish or plastic food bag.

Mix all the dry spices together in a jug or small bowl, then add all the remaining ingredients and stir until thoroughly combined.

Pour the marinade over the prepared meat, poultry, or fish and turn to coat.

Cover tightly or seal and leave to marinate in the refrigerator, turning occasionally, for up to 2 hours for fish or 4–6 hours or overnight for meat and poultry before cooking.

Spicy Beer Marinade

This gutsy marinade goes particularly well with beef, venison and wild boar, and the beer in the marinade makes it wonderfully tender as well as flavoursome.

Makes enough for about 500 g/1 lb 2 oz meat or game

350 ml/12 fl oz beer
100 ml/3½ fl oz soy sauce
1 tbsp Worcestershire sauce
1 tsp Tabasco sauce
1 garlic clove, finely chopped
1 tbsp wholegrain mustard
2 tsp paprika
1 tsp salt
1 tsp pepper

Score the meat or game portions deeply with a sharp knife. Put the prepared meat or game in a shallow non-metallic dish or plastic food bag.

Mix all the ingredients together in a jug or small bowl until thoroughly combined.

Pour the marinade over the prepared meat or game and turn to coat.

Cover tightly or seal and leave to marinate in the refrigerator, turning occasionally, for up to 6 hours before cooking.

Teriyaki Marinade

This Japanese-style marinade is perfect for use with salmon and trout fillets, chicken, duck and beef steaks.

Makes enough for about 500 g/1 lb 2 oz meat, poultry or fish

125 ml/4 fl oz dark soy sauce
200 ml/7 fl oz mirin or pale dry sherry
1 tbsp soft light brown sugar

Score the meat, poultry or fish portions deeply with a sharp knife. Put the prepared meat, poultry or fish in a shallow non-metallic dish or plastic food bag.

Heat all the ingredients in a large frying pan over a medium heat, stirring until the sugar has dissolved. Remove from the heat and leave to cool.

Pour the marinade over the prepared meat, poultry or fish and turn to coat.

Cover tightly or seal and leave to marinate in the refrigerator, turning occasionally, for up to 24 hours before cooking.

RUBS

Rubs are the dry equivalent of marinades and consist of a mixture of dried herbs and/or spices, salt and/or sugar. They are rubbed into raw food either just before cooking or up to 24 hours ahead. If leaving for the maximum length of time, you shouldn't add salt until just before cooking, otherwise moisture will be drawn out of the food and the result will be dry.

Rubs made up of dry ingredients keep extremely well in an airtight container, although you should avoid storing them for longer than 3 months as ground spices will begin to lose their flavour.

BBQ Spice Rub

This is an essential barbecue rub recipe and it is a delicious blend of spices that will add a rich, deep flavour to any meat dish, such as steaks, chops, sausages or spare ribs. It is also particularly good when used with thick cuts of fish.

Makes about 9 tbsp
4 tbsp soft dark brown sugar
1 tbsp mustard powder
1 tbsp salt
1 tbsp pepper
2 tsp paprika
1 tsp dried thyme
1 tsp dried oregano
1 tsp cayenne pepper
1 tsp ground allspice

Mix all the ingredients together in a small bowl until thoroughly combined.

Rub the mixture thoroughly into meat, poultry or fish just before cooking, if short of time, or up to 24 hours before cooking. If leaving for the maximum length of time, exclude the salt from the rub mixture and sprinkle over just before cooking.

Put in a shallow dish, cover tightly and chill in the refrigerator until required.

Cajun Blackened Spice Rub

The concept of 'blackening' food was created in New Orleans. As the food cooks, the spices form a delicious caramelized crust. This recipe is excellent with meat, poultry, firm fish steaks, such as salmon or swordfish, or large peeled and deveined prawns.

Makes about 4 tbsp
1 tbsp cracked black peppercorns
2 tsp paprika
2 tsp garlic powder or crushed garlic
2 tsp salt
1 tsp dried thyme
1 tsp dried oregano
1 tsp mustard powder
½ tsp cayenne pepper

Mix all the ingredients together in a small bowl until thoroughly combined.

Rub the mixture thoroughly into meat, poultry, fish or seafood just before cooking, if short of time, or for several hours before cooking.

Put in a shallow dish, cover tightly and chill in the refrigerator until required.

Jamaican Jerk Rub

Add a touch of Caribbean spice to your food with this exotic rub. It is a classic blend of allspice, thyme, nutmeg and cloves with a definite kick from the cayenne pepper. This is a great recipe to use with all types of meat and poultry, especially chicken.

Makes about 5 tbsp
4 tsp soft dark brown sugar
4 tsp chopped fresh thyme
4 tsp salt
2 tsp ground allspice
1 tsp cayenne pepper or chilli powder
generous pinch of freshly grated nutmeg
pinch of ground cloves

Mix all the ingredients together in a small bowl until thoroughly combined.

Rub the mixture thoroughly into meat, poultry, fish or seafood at least 2 hours, or up to 24 hours, before cooking. If leaving for the maximum length of time, exclude the salt from the rub mixture and sprinkle over just before cooking.

Put in a shallow dish, cover tightly and chill in the refrigerator until required.

Mediterranean Herb Rub

The fresh, bold flavours of the aromatic herbs and citrus rind in this recipe make this a perfect rub for use with all types of meat, poultry, fish and seafood, such as seabass, squid and scallops.

Makes about 10 tbsp
finely grated rind of 1 orange
finely grated rind of 1 lemon
3 garlic cloves, crushed
4 tbsp chopped fresh rosemary
2 tbsp chopped fresh sage
1 tbsp chopped fresh thyme
1 tbsp salt
2 tsp pepper

Mix all the ingredients together in a small bowl until thoroughly combined.

Rub the mixture thoroughly into meat, poultry, fish or seafood at least 2 hours, or up to 24 hours, before cooking. If leaving for the maximum length of time, exclude the salt from the rub mixture and sprinkle over just before cooking.

Put in a shallow non-metallic dish, cover tightly and chill in the refrigerator until required.

Texan-style Rub

This is a tasty and mildly spicy rub that is perfectly characteristic of the flavours popular in Texas for barbecuing spare ribs and steaks.

Makes about 5 tbsp
1 tbsp ground dried mild chillies
1 tbsp onion powder
1 tbsp mustard powder
1 tbsp salt

Mix all the ingredients together in a small bowl until thoroughly combined.

Rub the mixture thoroughly into meat, poultry, fish or seafood just before cooking, if short of time, or up to 24 hours before cooking. If leaving for the maximum length of time, exclude the salt from the rub mixture and sprinkle over just before cooking.

Put in a shallow dish, cover tightly and chill in the refrigerator until required.

Habanero Chilli Rub

Creole Rub

This intensely hot rub will give meat, such as tasty beef and red onion kebabs, and poultry a rich, powerful, almost fruity flavour. But be warned – it is very, very hot!

Makes about 10 tbsp
2 tbsp paprika
1–2 tbsp dried crushed habanero chillies
1 tbsp garlic powder
1 tbsp onion powder
1 tbsp ground cumin
1 tbsp salt
2 tsp pepper
2 tsp soft light brown sugar
1 tsp cayenne pepper
$^1/_2$ tsp freshly grated nutmeg

Mix all the ingredients together in a small bowl until thoroughly combined.

Rub the mixture thoroughly into the meat, poultry, fish or seafood 1–2 hours before cooking.

Put in a shallow dish, cover tightly and chill in the refrigerator until required.

This rub features vibrant Creole flavours and will perk up your taste buds. It is particularly delicious when used with fish and seafood.

Makes about 10 tbsp
2 tbsp pepper
2 tbsp celery salt
2 tbsp paprika
4 tsp garlic powder
4 tsp dried thyme
2 tsp dried oregano
2 tsp ground bay leaves
pinch of chilli powder

Mix all the ingredients together in a small bowl until thoroughly combined.

Rub the mixture thoroughly into meat, poultry, fish or seafood 1–2 hours before cooking.

Put in a shallow dish, cover tightly and chill in the refrigerator until required.

MEAT

CLASSIC CHEESE BURGERS

Place the beef in a large mixing bowl. Crumble the stock cube over the meat, add the dried onion and water and mix well. Divide the meat into 4 portions, shape each into a ball, then flatten slightly to make a burger shape of your preferred thickness.

Preheat the barbecue. Lightly brush the burgers with the oil and cook over hot coals for 5–6 minutes. Turn the burgers, sprinkle the cheese over the cooked side and cook for a further 5–6 minutes, until cooked through.

Place the lettuce leaves on the bottom halves of the buns and top with the burgers. Place a couple of tomato slices on top and add the lids. Serve immediately with chips.

SERVES 4

750 g/1 lb 10 oz fresh beef mince

1 beef stock cube

1 tbsp minced dried onion

2 tbsp water

1–2 tbsp sunflower oil

55 g/2 oz Cheddar cheese, grated

to serve

lettuce leaves

hamburger buns, split

tomato slices

chips

STEAK WITH ROCKET & PARMESAN

SERVES 4

4 sirloin steaks, 3 cm/1¼ inches
thick, about 225 g/8 oz each

olive oil, for greasing

100 g/3½ oz rocket

salt and pepper

grated Parmesan cheese and
balsamic vinegar, to serve

Preheat the barbecue to high. Snip the fat on the steaks at
1-cm/½-inch intervals to stop it curling and shrinking as it cooks.
Sprinkle both sides with salt and pepper. Cover and leave to
stand at room temperature for 30 minutes.

Heap some of the coals on one side leaving a slightly cooler
area with a single layer of coals. Oil the barbecue rack.

Cook the steaks on the hottest part of the grill for 2–3 minutes
on each side until brown. Move to the cooler part of the barbecue
and cook to your liking: rare 2½ minutes, medium–rare
3–3½ minutes and medium 4 minutes. Transfer to a board and
leave to rest for 5 minutes.

Carve each steak into 2 cm/¾ inch thick slices and transfer to
individual serving plates. Divide the rocket among the plates.
Sprinkle over the Parmesan, drizzle with balsamic vinegar and
serve immediately.

BEEF WITH WILD MUSHROOMS

Preheat the barbecue. Place the steaks on a chopping board and using a sharp knife, cut a pocket into the side of each steak.

To make the stuffing, heat the butter in a large frying pan. Add the garlic and fry gently for 1 minute. Add the mushrooms to the frying pan and sauté gently for 4–6 minutes, or until tender. Remove the frying pan from the heat and stir in the parsley.

Divide the mushroom mixture into 4 and insert a portion into the pocket of each steak. Seal the pocket with a cocktail stick. If preparing ahead, allow the mixture to cool before stuffing the steaks.

Cook the steaks over hot coals, searing the meat over the hottest part of the barbecue for 2 minutes on each side. Move the steaks to an area with slightly less intense heat and barbecue for a further 4–10 minutes on each side, depending on how well done you like your steaks.

Transfer the steaks to serving plates and remove the cocktail sticks. Serve immediately with salad leaves and cherry tomatoes.

SERVES 4

4 beef steaks

50 g/1¾ oz butter

1–2 garlic cloves, crushed

150 g/5½ oz mixed wild mushrooms

2 tbsp chopped fresh parsley

salad leaves and halved cherry tomatoes, to serve

SICHUAN PEPPERED STEAK

Place the steaks between 2 sheets of clingfilm and pound with a meat mallet until flattened to 5 mm/¼ inch. Slice each steak in half and place in a single layer in a shallow dish.

To make the marinade, place the garlic and salt in a mortar and pound with a pestle. Add both types of peppercorn, the sugar and chilli, and pound to a paste. Stir in the soy sauce and lime juice. Pour over the meat, turning to coat. Cover with clingfilm and leave to marinate at room temperature for 1 hour, or preferably overnight in the refrigerator.

Preheat the barbecue to medium–hot. Arrange the Chinese leaves, mint and coriander leaves in a shallow serving dish. Scatter with the onion slices and sprinkle with salt, pepper and lime juice to taste.

Remove the meat from the marinade, scraping off any solids and discarding the marinade. Pat dry with kitchen paper and lightly brush with oil. Thread concertina-style onto 4 metal or pre-soaked wooden skewers. Oil the grill rack.

Cook the meat over medium–hot coals for 3–4 minutes on each side, until browned. Transfer to a dish, remove the skewers and leave to rest for 5 minutes. Arrange on top of the salad and sprinkle with any juices from the meat. Serve immediately, garnished with the lime wedges.

SERVES 4

4 flank steaks or thin rump steaks,
   about 175 g/6 oz each
½ head Chinese leaves,
   thinly sliced
25 g/1 oz fresh mint leaves
25 g/1 oz fresh coriander leaves
½ red onion, thinly sliced
squeeze of lime juice
oil, for greasing
salt and pepper
lime wedges, to garnish

marinade
1 whole garlic bulb, cloves peeled
   and separated
¼ tsp salt
2 tbsp Sichuan peppercorns
1 tbsp black peppercorns
2 tsp soft brown sugar
1 fresh bird's eye chilli, deseeded
   and finely chopped
4 tbsp soy sauce
juice of 1 lime

BLT BURGERS WITH ASPARAGUS

SERVES 4–6

225 g/8 oz back bacon rashers

450 g/1 lb fresh steak mince

1 onion, grated

2–4 garlic cloves, crushed

1–2 tbsp sunflower oil

salt and pepper

dip

175 g/6 oz baby asparagus spears

1 tbsp lemon juice

1 small ripe avocado, peeled, stoned and finely chopped

2 firm tomatoes, peeled, deseeded and finely chopped

150 ml/5 fl oz crème fraîche

salt and pepper

to serve

lettuce leaves

hamburger buns, split

tomato slices

Remove any rind and fat from the bacon rashers and chop finely.

Place the bacon, steak mince, onion, garlic and salt and pepper in a large bowl and mix well. Shape into 4–6 equal-sized burgers, then cover and leave to chill in the refrigerator for 30 minutes.

To make the dip, trim the asparagus and cook in a saucepan of lightly salted boiling water for 5 minutes, then drain and plunge into cold water. When cold, drain and finely chop half the spears into a bowl and reserve the rest to serve. Sprinkle the lemon juice over the avocado. Stir in the avocado, tomatoes and crème fraîche. Add salt and pepper to taste, cover and leave to chill until required.

Preheat the barbecue. Lightly brush the burgers with the oil and cook over hot coals for 3–4 minutes on each side, or until cooked to personal preference.

Place the lettuce leaves on the bottom halves of the hamburger buns and top with the burgers. Top with a tomato slice, an asparagus spear and a spoonful of the dip. Add the lids and serve immediately.

HERB-CRUSTED
BEEF FILLET

Put the meat in a shallow dish and brush all over with the oil.
Sprinkle with the sea salt, peppercorns and herbs, rubbing in
well. Cover and leave to marinate in the refrigerator for 2 hours.

To make the horseradish butter, mash the butter with a fork
until soft, then add the remaining ingredients, mixing well.
Scrape the mixture onto a sheet of clingfilm and form into a log.
Wrap tightly and chill in the refrigerator.

Preheat the barbecue. Push some of the coals to one side to
make a slightly cooler coal-free area. Oil the grill rack.

Cook the meat over medium–hot coals for 8 minutes, giving
it a quarter-turn every 2 minutes, until brown and crusty on
the outside. Move to the cooler part of the barbecue and cover
with a lid. Cook for 16–18 minutes for rare or 20–25 minutes for
medium-rare.

Transfer the meat to a board. Cover with foil and leave for
15 minutes. Carve into 1 cm/½ inch diagonal slices and arrange
on warmed serving plates. Serve immediately with the juices
from the meat and slices of the horseradish butter.

SERVES 4

1 beef fillet, about 1 kg/2 lb 4 oz

1 tbsp olive oil, plus extra for
    greasing

½ tbsp sea salt

1 tsp coarsely ground peppercorns

4 tbsp chopped fresh mixed herbs,
    such as marjoram, thyme, sage
    and flat-leaf parsley

horseradish butter

100 g/3½ oz unsalted butter,
    at room temperature

3 tbsp grated fresh horseradish,
    or grated horseradish from a jar

salt and pepper

BOOZY BEEF STEAKS

Snip the fat on the steaks at ½-inch/1-cm intervals to stop it curling and shrinking as it cooks. Place the meat in a shallow, non-metallic dish.

Mix the whisky, soy sauce, sugar and pepper to taste together in a small bowl, stirring until the sugar dissolves. Pour the mixture over the steak. Cover with clingfilm and leave to marinate in the refrigerator for at least 2 hours.

Preheat the barbecue. Cook the meat over hot coals, searing the meat over the hottest part of the barbecue for 2 minutes on each side.

Move the meat to an area with slightly less intense heat and cook for a further 4–10 minutes on each side, depending on how well done you like your steaks.

Lightly barbecue the tomato slices for 1–2 minutes. Transfer the meat and the tomatoes to serving plates. Garnish with parsley sprigs and serve immediately with garlic bread.

SERVES 4

4 beef steaks
4 tbsp whisky or brandy
2 tbsp soy sauce
1 tbsp dark muscovado sugar
tomato slices
pepper
fresh flat-leaf parsley sprigs, to garnish
garlic bread, to serve

STEAK WITH PARSLEY BUTTER

SERVES 6

6 rump, sirloin or fillet steaks,
    about 175–225 g/6–8 oz

olive or sunflower oil, for greasing

pepper

baked potatoes and green salad,
    to serve

parsley butter

115 g/4 oz butter

3 tbsp finely chopped fresh
    parsley

1 tbsp lemon juice

salt and pepper

To make the parsley butter, put the butter into a bowl and beat with a wooden spoon until softened. Add the parsley and lemon juice, season to taste with salt and pepper and blend together until well mixed. Turn out onto a sheet of greaseproof paper and shape into a roll. Wrap in the greaseproof paper and leave to chill in the refrigerator for 2–3 hours, until firm.

Preheat the barbecue. If the steaks have a piece of fat running along them, cut or snip into it at regular intervals to prevent the steaks from curling and shrinking as they cook. Brush each steak with oil and season to taste with pepper. Cook the steaks over medium-hot coals for 2½ minutes on each side for rare, 4 minutes each side for medium, and 6 minutes on each side for well done. Transfer to serving plates.

Cut the parsley butter into 6 slices, then place a slice on top of each steak. Serve immediately, accompanied by baked potatoes and green salad.

JAMAICAN JERK PORK FILLET

To make the marinade, dry-roast the allspice berries in a small frying pan for a few seconds until you smell the aroma. Using a mortar and pestle, grind to a powder with the cloves, cinnamon stick and nutmeg. Tip into a food processor or blender with the remaining marinade ingredients. Process to a thin paste for 2 minutes, scraping the sides frequently.

Trim the sinew from the pork fillets and pull off any silvery skin. Spread the marinade all over the fillets, rubbing it in well. Cover with clingfilm and leave to marinate in the refrigerator for 2 hours.

Place the fillets on a board. Brush the upward-facing surfaces with oil. Place 1 fillet on top of the other, oiled-side down, to make a sandwich. Tie neatly with string at 3.5-cm/1¼-inch intervals and brush all over with oil. Season to taste with salt and pepper. Cover and leave to stand at room temperature for 30 minutes.

Preheat the barbecue. Heap some of the coals on 1 side leaving a slightly cooler area with a single layer of coals. Oil the grill rack.

Cook the meat over hot coals for 8 minutes, giving it a quarter-turn every 2 minutes, until brown and crusty on the outside. Move to the cooler part of the barbecue and cover with a lid. Cook for 20–25 minutes, or until cooked through.

Transfer the meat to a board. Cover with foil and leave to stand for 10 minutes. Carve into 1-cm/½-inch diagonal slices and arrange on serving plates. Serve immediately with the juices from the meat.

SERVES 4–6

2 pork fillets of equal length, about 1 kg/2 lb 4 oz in total

vegetable oil, for greasing

salt and pepper

jerk marinade

3 tbsp allspice berries

3 cloves

2-cm/¾-inch piece cinnamon stick, broken

½ tsp freshly grated nutmeg

2 large garlic cloves

1–2 fresh red chillies, deseeded and finely chopped

large bunch of fresh chives, about 1½ oz/40 g, snipped

2 tsp sea salt

2 tbsp malt vinegar

2 tbsp soy sauce

1 tbsp rum

HOT & SPICY SPARE RIBS

Preheat the barbecue. Put the onion, garlic, ginger, chilli and soy sauce into a food processor and process to a paste. Transfer to a jug and stir in the lime juice, sugar and oil and season to taste with salt and pepper.

Place the spare ribs in a preheated wok or large, heavy-based saucepan and pour in the soy sauce mixture. Place on the hob and bring to the boil, then simmer over a low heat, stirring frequently, for 30 minutes. If the mixture appears to be drying out, add a little water.

Remove the spare ribs, reserving the sauce. Cook the ribs over medium-hot coals, turning and basting frequently with the sauce, for 20–30 minutes. Transfer to a large serving plate and serve immediately.

SERVES 4

1 onion, chopped

2 garlic cloves, chopped

2.5-cm/1-inch piece fresh ginger, sliced

1 fresh red chilli, deseeded and chopped

5 tbsp dark soy sauce

3 tbsp lime juice

1 tbsp palm or muscovado sugar

2 tbsp groundnut oil

1 kg/2 lb 4 oz pork spare ribs, separated

salt and pepper

PORK BURGERS WITH ORANGE MARINADE

SERVES 4–6

450 g/1 lb pork fillet,
    cut into small pieces

3 tbsp Seville orange marmalade

2 tbsp orange juice

1 tbsp balsamic vinegar

225 g/8 oz parsnips,
    cut into chunks

1 tbsp finely grated orange rind

2 garlic cloves, crushed

6 spring onions, finely chopped

1 courgette, grated

1 tbsp sunflower oil

salt and pepper

to serve
lettuce leaves

hamburger buns, split

Place the pork in a shallow dish. Place the marmalade, orange juice and vinegar in a small saucepan and heat, stirring, until the marmalade is runny. Pour the marinade over the pork. Cover and leave for at least 30 minutes. Remove the pork, reserving the marinade. Mince the pork into a large bowl.

Meanwhile, cook the parsnips in a saucepan of boiling water for 15–20 minutes, or until tender. Drain, then mash and add to the pork. Stir in the orange rind, garlic, spring onions, courgette and salt and pepper to taste. Mix together, then shape into 4–6 equal-sized burgers. Cover and leave to chill for at least 30 minutes.

Preheat the barbecue. Lightly brush each burger with the oil and then add them to the barbecue grill, cooking over medium–hot coals for 4–6 minutes on each side, or until cooked through. Boil the reserved marinade for at least 5 minutes, then pour into a small jug or bowl.

Place the lettuce leaves on the bottom halves of the hamburger buns and top with the burgers. Spoon over a little of the hot marinade, then top with the lids and serve immediately.

MEATBALLS ON STICKS

Preheat the barbecue. Remove the sausage meat from the skins, place in a large bowl and break up with a fork. Add the beef mince, breadcrumbs, onion, herbs and egg. Season to taste with salt and pepper and stir well with a wooden spoon until thoroughly mixed.

Form the mixture into small balls, about the size of a golf ball, between the palms of your hands. Spear each meatball with a cocktail stick and brush with oil.

Cook over medium–hot coals, turning frequently and brushing with more oil as necessary, for 10 minutes, or until cooked through. Serve immediately.

SERVES 8

4 pork and herb sausages

115 g/4 oz fresh beef mince

85 g/3 oz fresh white breadcrumbs

1 onion, finely chopped

2 tbsp chopped mixed fresh herbs, such as parsley, thyme and sage

1 egg

sunflower oil, for greasing

salt and pepper

SPICY PORK SAUSAGES

Put the garlic, onion, chilli, pork, almonds, breadcrumbs and chopped thyme into a large bowl. Season well with salt and pepper and mix until well combined.

Using your hands, form the mixture into sausage shapes. Roll each sausage in a little flour, then transfer to a bowl, cover with clingfilm and refrigerate for 45 minutes.

Preheat the barbecue. Brush a piece of foil with oil, then put the sausages on the foil and brush them with a little more oil. Transfer the sausages and foil to the barbecue. Cook over hot coals, turning the sausages frequently, for about 15 minutes, or until cooked through.

Split the hot dog rolls down the centre and insert a layer of fried onions and lettuce leaves. Place the sausages in the rolls and serve immediately with ketchup, garnished with thyme sprigs.

SERVES 4

1 garlic clove, finely chopped

1 onion, grated

1 small fresh red chilli, deseeded and finely chopped

450 g/1 lb lean minced pork

50 g/1¾ oz almonds, toasted and ground

50 g/1¾ oz fresh breadcrumbs

1 tbsp finely chopped fresh thyme, plus extra sprigs to garnish

flour, for dusting

vegetable oil, for greasing

salt and pepper

to serve

hot dog rolls

fried onions

lettuce leaves

tomato ketchup and/or mustard

PORK KEBABS WITH SWEET CHILLI SAUCE

SERVES 4

1 large onion, chopped

2 garlic cloves, crushed

450 g/1 lb fresh pork mince

1 tsp salt

2 tbsp sweet chilli sauce, plus extra to serve

handful of fresh coriander, chopped

1 egg

sunflower oil, for greasing

egg-fried rice, to serve

Put all the ingredients except the rice in a food processor and process to a thick paste.

Divide the pork mixture into 8 portions. Using damp hands, squeeze each portion evenly around a metal or pre-soaked wooden skewer to form a sausage shape. Cover and chill in the refrigerator for at least 1 hour.

Preheat the barbecue. Cook the kebabs over medium–hot coals, turning frequently, for 15 minutes, or until browned all over and cooked through. Serve immediately with egg-fried rice and sweet chilli sauce.

LEMON &
HERB PORK
ESCALOPES

Place the pork escalopes in a large, shallow, non-metallic dish.
Heat the oil in a small, heavy-based saucepan. Add the bay
leaves and stir-fry for 1 minute. Stir in the lemon rind and juice,
beer, honey and juniper berries and season to taste with salt
and pepper.

Pour the mixture over the pork, turning to coat. Cover with
clingfilm, leave to cool and chill in the refrigerator for up to
8 hours.

Preheat the barbecue. Drain the pork, reserving the marinade.
Core the apple and cut into rings. Cook the pork over medium–
hot coals, brushing frequently with the reserved marinade, for
5 minutes on each side, or until thoroughly cooked. Cook the
apple rings on the barbecue, brushing frequently with the
marinade, for 3 minutes. Transfer the pork to a large serving
plate with the apple rings and serve immediately.

SERVES 4

4 pork escalopes

2 tbsp sunflower oil

6 fresh bay leaves, torn into
    pieces

grated rind and juice of 2 lemons

125 ml/4 fl oz beer

1 tbsp clear honey

6 juniper berries, lightly crushed

1 crisp dessert apple

salt and pepper

HONEY-GLAZED PORK CHOPS

Preheat the barbecue. Season the pork chops with salt and
pepper to taste. Reserve while you make the glaze.

To make the glaze, place the honey, sherry, orange juice, olive
oil, and ginger in a small pan and heat gently, stirring constantly,
until well blended.

Grease the grill rack. Cook the pork chops over hot coals for
5 minutes on each side. Brush the chops with the glaze and cook
for an additional 2–4 minutes on each side, basting frequently
with the glaze.

Transfer the pork chops to warmed serving plates and
serve immediately.

SERVES 4

4 lean pork loin chops

4 tbsp honey

1 tbsp dry sherry

4 tbsp orange juice

2 tbsp olive oil

1-inch/2.5-cm piece fresh ginger,
grated

sunflower oil, for greasing

salt and pepper

SPICED LAMB & APRICOT KEBABS

SERVES 6

675 g/1 lb 8 oz boneless lamb, cut into 2.5-cm/1-inch cubes

12 ready-to-eat dried apricots, halved lengthways

6 baby onions, quartered lengthways

18 fresh bay leaves

oil, for greasing

marinade

4 tbsp vegetable oil

2 onions, finely chopped

4 garlic cloves, finely chopped

2 tbsp curry powder

2 tsp garam masala

½ tsp cayenne pepper

2 tbsp muscovado sugar

1 tsp salt

1 tsp pepper

4 tbsp white wine vinegar

5 tbsp apricot jam

200 ml/7 fl oz water

First make the marinade. Heat the oil in a frying pan over a medium heat. Add the onions and cook gently for 10 minutes or until browned. Add the garlic, curry powder, garam masala and cayenne pepper, and continue frying for 30 seconds. Stir in the sugar, salt, pepper, vinegar, apricot jam and half the water. Simmer, stirring for 2–3 minutes, or until the marinade thickens. Remove from the heat and leave to cool completely.

Put the lamb in a bowl with the cold marinade, stirring to coat. Cover with clingfilm and leave to marinate in the refrigerator for at least 4 hours or overnight.

Preheat the barbecue. Remove the meat from the marinade, reserving the marinade. Thread the meat onto 6 metal or pre-soaked wooden skewers, alternating with the apricots, baby onions and bay leaves, and brush with oil. Grease the grill rack. Cook over medium–hot coals, turning occasionally and brushing with more oil, for 15 minutes, until cooked through.

Place the reserved marinade in a small pan with the remaining water. Boil for 5 minutes, stirring constantly, until thickened. Serve the kebabs immediately with the hot marinade.

SPICY LAMB STEAKS

To make the marinade, heat the sunflower oil in a heavy-based saucepan. Add the onion and garlic and cook, stirring occasionally, for 5 minutes, or until softened. Stir in the jerk seasoning, curry paste and ginger and cook, stirring constantly, for 2 minutes. Add the tomatoes, Worcestershire sauce and sugar, then season to taste with salt and pepper. Bring to the boil, stirring constantly, then reduce the heat and simmer for 15 minutes, or until thickened. Remove from the heat and leave to cool.

Place the lamb steaks between 2 sheets of clingfilm and beat with the side of a rolling pin to flatten. Transfer the steaks to a large, shallow, non-metallic dish. Pour the marinade over them, turning to coat. Cover with clingfilm and leave to marinate in the refrigerator for 3 hours.

Preheat the barbecue. Drain the lamb, reserving the marinade. Cook the lamb over medium–hot coals, brushing frequently with the marinade, for 5–7 minutes on each side. Meanwhile, dip the rosemary and bay leaves in the olive oil and cook on the barbecue for 3–5 minutes. Serve the lamb immediately with the herbs.

SERVES 4

4 lamb steaks, about 175 g/6 oz each

8 fresh rosemary sprigs

8 fresh bay leaves

2 tbsp olive oil

spicy marinade

2 tbsp sunflower oil

1 large onion, finely chopped

2 garlic cloves, finely chopped

2 tbsp jerk seasoning

1 tbsp curry paste

1 tsp grated fresh ginger

400 g/14 oz canned chopped tomatoes

4 tbsp Worcestershire sauce

3 tbsp light muscovado sugar

salt and pepper

LAMB & FETA BURGERS

Place the lamb mince in a large bowl with the feta, garlic, spring onions, prunes, pine kernels and breadcrumbs. Mix well, breaking up any lumps of mince.

Add the rosemary to the lamb mixture with salt and pepper to taste. Mix together, then shape into 4–6 equal-sized burgers. Cover and leave to chill for 30 minutes.

Preheat the barbecue. Brush the burgers lightly with half the oil and cook over hot coals for 4 minutes, then brush with the remaining oil and turn over. Continue to cook for 4 minutes, or until cooked through. Serve immediately.

SERVES 4–6

450 g/1 lb fresh lamb mince

225 g/8 oz feta cheese, crumbled

2 garlic cloves, crushed

6 spring onions, finely chopped

85 g/3 oz ready-to-eat prunes, chopped

25 g/1 oz pine kernels, toasted

55 g/2 oz fresh wholemeal breadcrumbs

1 tbsp chopped fresh rosemary

1 tbsp sunflower oil

salt and pepper

INDIAN KOFTAS

SERVES 4

1 small onion
450 g/1 lb fresh lean lamb mince
2 tbsp curry paste
2 tbsp natural yogurt
sunflower oil, for greasing
poppadoms and chutney, to serve

tomato sambal
3 tomatoes, deseeded and diced
pinch of ground coriander
pinch of ground cumin
2 tsp chopped fresh coriander
salt and pepper

Place the onion in a food processor and chop finely. Add the lamb and process briefly to chop further. Alternatively, grate the onion finely before mixing it with the lamb.

Add the curry paste and yogurt and mix well. Divide the mixture into 8 equal-sized portions. Press and shape the mixture into 8 sausage shapes and push each onto a metal or pre-soaked wooden skewer, pressing the mixture together firmly so that it holds its shape. Leave to chill in the refrigerator for at least 30 minutes, or until required.

To make the tomato sambal, mix the tomatoes, spices, coriander and salt and pepper to taste together in a bowl. Leave to stand for at least 30 minutes for the flavours to combine.

Preheat the barbecue. Grease the grill rack. Cook the kebabs over hot coals, turning frequently and brushing with a little oil if needed, for 10–15 minutes, until cooked through. Serve accompanied by poppadoms, chutney and the tomato sambal.

MOROCCAN LAMB BURGERS

To make the sauce, peel the cucumber, quarter lengthways and scoop out the seeds. Chop the flesh and put in a sieve set over a bowl. Sprinkle with salt, cover with a plate and weigh down with a can of vegetables. Leave to drain for 30 minutes, then mix with the remaining ingredients.

Combine the lamb, onion, harissa sauce, garlic, mint, cumin seeds and paprika. Season to taste with salt and pepper, mixing well with a fork. Divide into 4 balls and flatten into patties about 2.5 cm/1 inch thick. Cover and leave to stand at room temperature for 30 minutes.

Preheat the barbecue. Lightly brush the burgers with oil. Grease the grill rack. Cook over hot coals for 5–6 minutes on each side, or until cooked through.

Stuff the burgers into warmed pitta breads with the red onion, lettuce and a spoonful of the sauce. Serve immediately.

SERVES 4

550 g/1 lb 4 oz fresh lamb mince

1 onion, grated

1 tsp harissa sauce

1 garlic clove, crushed

2 tbsp finely chopped fresh mint

½ tsp cumin seeds, crushed

½ tsp paprika

oil, for greasing

salt and pepper

yogurt & cucumber sauce

½ large cucumber

4 tbsp natural yogurt

6 tbsp chopped fresh mint

salt

to serve

4 pitta breads, warmed

½ red onion, halved and thinly sliced

shredded lettuce

LAMB RACKS WITH ROSEMARY

Place the lamb in a large, shallow, non-metallic dish. Place the oil, vinegar, lemon juice, rosemary and onion in a jug and stir together. Season to taste with salt and pepper.

Pour the marinade over the lamb and turn until thoroughly coated. Cover with clingfilm and leave to marinate in the refrigerator for 1 hour, turning occasionally.

Preheat the barbecue. Drain the racks of lamb, reserving the marinade. Cook over medium–hot coals, brushing frequently with the marinade, for 10 minutes on each side. Garnish with the rosemary sprigs and serve immediately.

SERVES 4

4 racks of lamb, each with
  4 cutlets

2 tbsp extra virgin olive oil

1 tbsp balsamic vinegar

1 tbsp lemon juice

3 tbsp finely chopped fresh
  rosemary, plus extra sprigs
  to garnish

1 small onion, finely chopped

salt and pepper

BUTTERFLIED LAMB WITH MINT

SERVES 4

1 boned leg of lamb,
  about 1.8 kg/4 lb

8 tbsp balsamic vinegar

grated rind and juice of 1 lemon

150 ml/5 fl oz sunflower oil

4 tbsp chopped fresh mint

2 garlic cloves, crushed

2 tbsp light muscovado sugar

salt and pepper

to serve
barbecued vegetables, such as
  peppers and courgettes

black or green olives

Open out the boned leg of lamb so that its shape resembles
a butterfly. Thread 2–3 metal or pre-soaked wooden skewers
through the meat to make it easier to turn on the barbecue.

Mix the vinegar, lemon rind and juice, oil, mint, garlic, sugar
and salt and pepper to taste together in a non-metallic dish that
is large enough to hold the lamb. Place the lamb in the dish and
turn it over a few times so that the meat is coated on both sides
with the marinade. Cover and leave to marinate in the refrigerator
for at least 6 hours, or preferably overnight, turning occasionally.

Preheat the barbecue. Drain the lamb, reserving the marinade.
Place the rack about 15 cm/6 inches above the coals and cook
the lamb for 30 minutes on each side, turning once and basting
frequently with the marinade.

Transfer the lamb to a chopping board and remove the
skewers. Cut the lamb into slices across the grain and serve with
barbecued vegetables and olives.

POULTRY

CAJUN CHICKEN

Preheat the barbecue. Using a sharp knife, make 2–3 diagonal slashes in the chicken drumsticks and thighs, then place them in a large dish. Cut the sweetcorn cobs into thick slices and add them to the dish. Mix all the ingredients for the spice mix together in a small bowl.

Brush the chicken and sweetcorn with the melted butter and sprinkle with the spice mix. Toss to coat well.

Cook the chicken over medium–hot coals, turning occasionally, for 15 minutes, then add the sweetcorn slices and cook, turning occasionally, for a further 10–15 minutes, or until beginning to blacken slightly at the edges. Transfer to a large serving plate, garnish with the parsley and serve immediately.

SERVES 4

4 chicken drumsticks

4 chicken thighs

2 fresh sweetcorn cobs, husks and
    silks removed

85 g/3 oz butter, melted

fresh flat-leaf parsley sprigs,
    to garnish

spice mix
2 tsp onion powder

2 tsp paprika

1½ tsp salt

1 tsp garlic powder

1 tsp dried thyme

1 tsp cayenne pepper

1 tsp ground black pepper

½ tsp ground white pepper

¼ tsp ground cumin

CHICKEN KEBABS WITH LEMON & HERBS

Put the yogurt, garlic, lemon juice, herbs, and salt and pepper to taste in a large bowl and mix well together.

Cut the chicken breasts into 4-cm/1½-inch chunks. Add to the yogurt mixture and toss well together until the chicken pieces are coated. Cover and leave to marinate in the refrigerator for about 1 hour.

Preheat the barbecue. Drain the chicken, reserving the marinade. Thread the pieces of chicken onto 8 metal or pre-soaked wooden skewers. Cook the kebabs over medium–hot coals, turning and basting occasionally with the remaining marinade, for 15 minutes, or until cooked through.

Serve the kebabs on a bed of rice with the lettuce and lemon wedges for squeezing over.

SERVES 4

300 ml/10 fl oz Greek yogurt

2 garlic cloves, crushed

juice of ½ lemon

1 tbsp chopped fresh herbs such as oregano, dill, tarragon or parsley

4 large skinless, boneless chicken breasts

salt and pepper

to serve
cooked rice

shredded lettuce

lemon wedges

ITALIAN DEVILLED CHICKEN

SERVES 4

4 skinless, boneless chicken
    breasts, about 175 g/6 oz each,
    cut into 2.5-cm/1-inch cubes

125 ml/4 fl oz olive oil

finely grated rind and juice of
    1 lemon

2 garlic cloves, finely chopped

2 tsp finely chopped dried red
    chillies

salt and pepper

fresh flat-leaf parsley sprigs,
    to garnish

Place the chicken in a large, shallow, non-metallic dish. Place
the oil, lemon rind and juice, garlic and chillies in a jug and stir
together until well blended. Season to taste with salt and pepper.

Pour the mixture over the chicken and stir gently to coat.
Cover with clingfilm and leave to marinate in the refrigerator for
up to 8 hours.

Preheat the barbecue. Drain the chicken, reserving the
marinade. Thread the chicken onto 8 metal or pre-soaked
wooden skewers and cook over medium–hot coals, turning
and brushing frequently with the reserved marinade, for
6–10 minutes, or until cooked through. Transfer to a large
serving dish, garnish with parsley sprigs and serve immediately.

CHICKEN SATAY

Preheat the barbecue. Mix the peanut butter and soy sauce together in a bowl until smooth. Stir in the chicken strips, tossing well to coat in the mixture.

Thread the chicken strips onto 8 metal or pre-soaked wooden skewers. Cook over medium–hot coals for about 5 minutes on each side, or until cooked through. Serve immediately.

SERVES 4

4 tbsp smooth peanut butter

100 ml/3½ fl oz soy sauce

4 skinless, boneless chicken breasts, cut into thin strips

SPICY CHICKEN PITTA POCKETS

Place the chicken in a large bowl. Mix the yogurt, chilli powder, lime juice, coriander, green chilli and oil together in a jug with salt to taste. Pour the mixture over the chicken and toss until the chicken is coated. Cover with clingfilm and leave to marinate in the refrigerator for 2 hours.

Preheat the barbecue. Drain the chicken, reserving the marinade. Thread the chicken onto 4 metal or pre-soaked wooden skewers. Cook over medium–hot coals, turning and brushing frequently with the reserved marinade, for 6–10 minutes, or until cooked through. Meanwhile, slit the pitta breads with a sharp knife and toast briefly on the barbecue.

To serve, remove the chicken from the skewers and fill the pitta breads with the lettuce, tomato slices, spring onions and chicken. Top with the jalapeño chillies and serve immediately with lemon wedges for squeezing over.

SERVES 4

500 g/1 lb 2 oz skinless, boneless chicken, cut into 2.5-cm/1-inch cubes

3 tbsp natural yogurt

1 tsp chilli powder

3 tbsp lime juice

1 tbsp chopped fresh coriander

1 fresh green chilli, deseeded and finely chopped

1 tbsp sunflower oil

salt

to serve

4 pitta breads

¼ iceberg lettuce, shredded

2 tomatoes, thinly sliced

8 spring onions, chopped

8 bottled jalapeño chillies, drained

lemon wedges

BACON-WRAPPED CHICKEN BURGERS

SERVES 4

450 g/1 lb fresh chicken mince

1 onion, grated

2 garlic cloves, crushed

55 g/2 oz pine kernels, toasted

55 g/2 oz Gruyère cheese, grated

2 tbsp fresh snipped chives

2 tbsp wholemeal flour

8 lean back bacon rashers

1–2 tbsp sunflower oil

salt and pepper

to serve

shredded lettuce

sliced red onion

hamburger buns, split

soured cream

snipped fresh chives

Place the chicken mince, onion, garlic, pine kernels, cheese, chives and salt and pepper to taste in a food processor. Using the pulse button, blend the mixture together using short sharp bursts. Scrape out onto a board and shape into 4 equal-sized burgers. Coat in the flour, then cover and leave to chill in the refrigerator for 1 hour.

Wrap each burger with 2 bacon rashers, securing in place with a cocktail stick.

Preheat the barbecue. Brush the burgers with the oil and cook over medium-hot coals for 5–6 minutes on each side, or until cooked through. Remove and discard the cocktail sticks.

Place the shredded lettuce and onion on the bottom halves of the hamburger buns and top with the burgers. Spoon over a little soured cream and sprinkle with chives, add the lids and serve immediately.

ZESTY CHICKEN KEBABS

Using a sharp knife, cut the chicken into 2.5-cm/1-inch cubes, then place in a large glass bowl. Place the lemon and orange rind, the lemon and orange juice, the honey, oil, mint and coriander in a jug and mix together. Season to taste with salt and pepper. Pour the marinade over the chicken and toss until they are thoroughly coated. Cover with clingfilm and leave to marinate in the refrigerator for up to 8 hours.

Preheat the barbecue. Drain the chicken, reserving the marinade. Thread the chicken onto 8 metal or pre-soaked wooden skewers.

Cook the skewers over medium–hot coals, turning and brushing frequently with the reserved marinade, for 6–10 minutes, or until cooked through. Transfer to a large serving plate and serve immediately.

SERVES 4

4 skinless, boneless chicken breasts, about 175 g/6 oz each

finely grated rind and juice of ½ lemon

finely grated rind and juice of ½ orange

2 tbsp clear honey

2 tbsp olive oil

2 tbsp chopped fresh mint

¼ tsp ground coriander

salt and pepper

CHICKEN FAJITAS

Slice the chicken breasts horizontally in half to make 4–6 thinner pieces. Place between 2 sheets of clingfilm and pound with a meat mallet until flattened to a thickness of 5 mm/¼ inch. Place in a single layer in a shallow dish.

To make the marinade, place the garlic, chilli, cumin seeds and sugar in a mortar with salt and pepper to taste. Pound to a paste using a pestle. Transfer to a bowl and stir in the lime juice, vinegar and oil. Reserve 4 tablespoons of the marinade and set aside. Pour the remaining marinade over the chicken. Cover and leave to marinate in the refrigerator for 30 minutes.

Preheat the barbecue. Cut the onion into 3 thick slices. Insert cocktail sticks through each slice to keep the rings in place. Brush the onion and red peppers with oil and arrange in a hinged wire grill basket. Cook the vegetables over medium–hot coals, turning occasionally, for 8–12 minutes, until slightly charred. Slice the peppers into thin strips and remove the cocktail sticks from the onion slices. Tip the vegetables into a warmed bowl and toss with half the reserved marinade and half the coriander.

Drain the chicken, discarding the marinade. Grease the grill rack. Cook over medium–hot coals for 3–4 minutes on each side, or until cooked through. Slice into thin strips, put in a warmed bowl and toss with the remaining reserved marinade and coriander.

Warm the tortillas on the barbecue. Spoon a little soured cream down the centre of each tortilla and add some chicken and vegetables. Roll up and serve with the Avocado Salsa.

SERVES 4

2–3 skinless, boneless chicken breasts, about 450 g/1 lb in total

1 red onion

2 red or yellow peppers, deseeded and quartered lengthways

olive oil, for greasing

3 tbsp chopped fresh coriander

4 corn tortillas

soured cream and Avocado Salsa (see page 92), to serve

marinade

1 large garlic clove, crushed

½ –1 fresh green chilli, deseeded and finely chopped

½ tsp cumin seeds

1 tsp sugar

2 tbsp lime juice

2 tbsp white wine vinegar

4 tbsp olive oil

salt and pepper

SPICY CHICKEN
& TOMATO
KEBABS

SERVES 4

500 g/1 lb 2 oz skinless, boneless
   chicken breasts

3 tbsp tomato purée

2 tbsp clear honey

2 tbsp Worcestershire sauce

1 tbsp chopped fresh rosemary

250 g/9 oz cherry tomatoes

Using a sharp knife, cut the chicken into small chunks and place
in a bowl. Mix together the tomato purée, honey, Worcestershire
sauce and rosemary in a separate bowl, then add to the chicken,
stirring to coat evenly.

Preheat the barbecue. Drain the chicken, reserving the
marinade. Thread the chicken pieces and cherry tomatoes
alternately onto 8 metal or pre-soaked wooden skewers.

Cook the kebabs over medium–hot coals, turning occasionally
and basting with the reserved marinade, for 8–10 minutes, until
the chicken is cooked through. Transfer to a large plate and serve
immediately.

CHICKEN WITH TARRAGON BUTTER

Preheat the barbecue. To make the tarragon butter, mash the butter with a fork until soft, then add the tarragon, shallot and salt and pepper to taste, mixing well. Scrape the mixture onto a piece of clingfilm and form into a log. Wrap tightly and chill in the refrigerator.

Slice the chicken breasts lengthways to make 8 portions. Place in a single layer in a shallow dish. Mix together the marinade ingredients and pour over the chicken. Cover with clingfilm and leave to marinate in the refrigerator for 30 minutes, turning halfway through.

Drain the chicken, discarding the marinade. Pat dry and lightly brush with oil. Grease the grill rack. Place the chicken on the rack and cover with a disposable foil tray. Grill over medium–hot coals for 5–6 minutes, until the underside is striped with grill marks and is no longer translucent. Using tongs, turn and cook the other side for 4–5 minutes, or until cooked through.

Place in a warmed dish, cover with foil and leave to rest in a warm place for 5 minutes. Serve immediately with slices of the tarragon butter.

SERVES 4

4 skinless, boneless chicken breasts, about 225 g/8 oz each

oil, for greasing

tarragon butter
100 g/3½ oz unsalted butter, at room temperature

5 tbsp chopped fresh tarragon

1 shallot, finely chopped

salt and pepper

marinade
1½ tbsp lemon juice

2 tbsp water

1 tsp sugar

1 tsp salt

½ tsp pepper

3 tbsp olive oil

BUTTERFLIED POUSSINS

To butterfly the poussins, turn each bird breast-side down and, using strong kitchen scissors or poultry shears, cut through the skin and ribcage along both sides of the backbone, from tail to neck. Remove the backbone and turn the bird breast-side up. Press down firmly on the breastbone to flatten. Fold the wingtips underneath. Push a skewer through a wing, the top of the breast and out of the other wing. Push a second skewer through a thigh, the bottom of the breast and out through the other thigh.

Mix the paprika, mustard powder, cumin, cayenne, tomato ketchup and lemon juice together in a small bowl and season to taste with salt. Gradually stir in the butter to make a smooth paste. Spread the paste evenly over the poussins, cover and leave to marinate in the refrigerator for up to 8 hours.

Preheat the barbecue. Cook the poussins over medium–hot coals, turning frequently and brushing with a little oil if necessary for 25–30 minutes, or until cooked through. Transfer to a serving plate, garnish with coriander sprigs and serve immediately with sweetcorn cobs.

SERVES 4

4 poussins, about 450 g/1 lb each
1 tbsp paprika
1 tbsp mustard powder
1 tbsp ground cumin
pinch of cayenne pepper
1 tbsp tomato ketchup
1 tbsp lemon juice
5 tbsp melted butter
oil, for greasing
salt
fresh coriander sprigs, to garnish
cooked sweetcorn cobs,
    to serve

MEXICAN TURKEY BURGERS

SERVES 4

450 g/1 lb fresh turkey mince

200 g/7 oz canned refried beans

2–4 garlic cloves, crushed

1–2 fresh jalapeño chillies, deseeded and finely chopped

2 tbsp tomato purée

1 tbsp chopped fresh coriander

1 tbsp sunflower oil

salt and pepper

to serve

shredded baby spinach leaves

cheese-topped hamburger buns, split

salsa

guacamole (see page 265)

tortilla chips

Place the turkey mince in a bowl and break up any large lumps. Beat the refried beans until smooth, then add to the turkey in the bowl.

Add the garlic, chillies, tomato purée and coriander with salt and pepper to taste and mix together. Shape into 4 equal-sized burgers, then cover and leave to chill in the refrigerator for 1 hour.

Preheat the barbecue. Brush the burgers with the oil and cook over medium–hot coals for 5–6 minutes on each side, or until cooked through.

Place the spinach on the bottom halves of the hamburger buns and top with the burgers. Spoon over a little salsa and guacamole and top with the lids. Serve immediately with tortilla chips on the side.

TURKEY KEBABS WITH AVOCADO SALSA

Halve the turkey steaks horizontally to make 8 thinner pieces. Place between 2 sheets of clingfilm and pound with a meat mallet until flattened to a thickness of 1 cm/½ inch. Slice into strips about 4 cm/1½ inches wide and 6 cm/2½ inches long. Place in a single layer in a shallow dish.

Whisk together the marinade ingredients and pour over the turkey. Cover with clingfilm and leave to marinate in the refrigerator for at least 4 hours or overnight.

Preheat the barbecue. Carefully toss the salsa ingredients together and leave to stand at room temperature to allow the flavours to develop.

Drain the turkey, discarding the marinade. Lightly brush with oil and thread concertina-style onto 8 metal or pre-soaked wooden skewers. Grease the grill rack. Cook over hot coals for 2–2½ minutes on each side, or until cooked through. Remove from the skewers and serve immediately with the avocado salsa and warmed tortillas.

SERVES 4

4 turkey steaks, 500 g/1 lb 2 oz in total

olive oil, for greasing

warmed flour tortillas, to serve

marinade

juice of 1 orange

juice of 2 limes

2 garlic cloves, crushed

1 tsp paprika

½ tsp salt

½ tsp chilli powder

½ tsp cumin seeds, crushed

¼ tsp pepper

4 tbsp olive oil

avocado salsa

2 avocados, stoned, peeled and finely chopped

juice of 1 lime

1 small red onion, finely diced

1 tbsp chopped fresh coriander

salt

TURKEY TIKKA KEBABS

Cut the turkey into cubes and put in a shallow dish. Combine the salt, pepper, cayenne and lemon juice in a small bowl and pour over the turkey, turning to coat. Cover with clingfilm and leave to stand for 30 minutes.

Process the marinade ingredients to a paste in a blender or food processor. Mix with the turkey, making sure the cubes are well coated. Cover and leave to marinate in the refrigerator for at least 2 hours or overnight.

Preheat the barbecue. Thread the turkey cubes onto 4 metal or pre-soaked wooden skewers, alternating them with the bay leaves and onion quarters. Brush with oil on all sides. Grease the grill rack.

Cook the kebabs over medium–hot coals, turning occasionally, for 10–12 minutes, until the turkey is cooked through and slightly charred at the edges. Transfer to a serving plate, sprinkle with the coriander and serve immediately.

SERVES 4

4 turkey steaks, 500 g/1 lb 2 oz in total

½ tsp salt

½ tsp pepper

½–1 tsp cayenne pepper

juice of ½ lemon

12 fresh bay leaves

4 small red onions, quartered lengthways

oil, for greasing

1 tbsp chopped fresh coriander

marinade

175 g/6 oz Greek-style yogurt

5-cm/2-inch piece fresh ginger, chopped

1 tsp garam masala

½–1 tsp cayenne pepper

1 tsp salt

juice of ½ lemon

4 tbsp vegetable oil

TURKEY & TARRAGON BURGERS

SERVES 4

55 g/2 oz bulgar wheat

450 g/1 lb fresh turkey mince

1 tbsp finely grated orange rind

1 red onion, finely chopped

1 yellow pepper, deseeded, peeled and finely chopped

25 g/1 oz toasted flaked almonds

1 tbsp chopped fresh tarragon

1–2 tbsp sunflower oil

salt and pepper

to serve

lettuce leaves

2 baked potatoes, halved

tomato relish

tomato and onion salad

Cook the bulgar wheat in a saucepan of lightly salted boiling water for 10–15 minutes, or according to the packet instructions.

Drain the bulgar wheat and place in a bowl with the turkey mince, orange rind, onion, yellow pepper, almonds, tarragon and salt and pepper to taste. Mix together, then shape into 4 equal-sized burgers. Cover and leave to chill in the refrigerator for 1 hour.

Preheat the barbecue. Brush the burgers with the oil and cook over medium–hot coals for 5–6 minutes on each side, or until cooked through.

Put a few lettuce leaves on 4 serving plates and place a baked potato half on top of each. Top with the burgers, spoon over a little relish and serve immediately with a tomato and onion salad.

POULTRY

97

TARRAGON
TURKEY

Preheat the barbecue. Season the turkey to taste with salt and pepper, and, using a round-bladed knife, spread the mustard evenly over the turkey.

Place 2 tarragon sprigs on top of each turkey breast and wrap a bacon rasher around it to hold the tarragon in place. Secure with a cocktail stick.

Cook the turkey over medium–hot coals for 5–8 minutes on each side, or until cooked through. Transfer to serving plates and garnish with tarragon sprigs. Serve immediately with salad leaves.

SERVES 4

4 turkey steaks, about
175 g/6 oz each

4 tsp wholegrain mustard

8 fresh tarragon sprigs,
plus extra to garnish

4 smoked back bacon rashers

salt and pepper

salad leaves, to serve

TURKEY WITH CORIANDER PESTO

Place the turkey in a large glass bowl. To make the marinade, mix the olive oil, wine, peppercorns and coriander together in a jug with salt to taste. Pour the mixture over the turkey and toss until the turkey is thoroughly coated. Cover with clingfilm and leave to marinate in the refrigerator for 2 hours.

Preheat the barbecue. To make the pesto, put the coriander and parsley into a food processor and process until finely chopped. Add the garlic and pine kernels and pulse until chopped. Add the Parmesan cheese, extra virgin olive oil and lemon juice and process briefly to mix. Transfer to a bowl, cover and leave to chill in the refrigerator until required.

Drain the turkey, reserving the marinade. Thread the turkey, courgette slices, pepper pieces, cherry tomatoes and onions alternately onto 8 metal or pre-soaked wooden skewers. Cook over medium–hot coals, turning and brushing frequently with the marinade, for 10 minutes, or until cooked through. Serve immediately with the coriander pesto.

SERVES 4

450 g/1 lb turkey steaks, cut into 5-cm/2-inch cubes

2 courgettes, thickly sliced

1 red and 1 yellow pepper, deseeded and cut into 5-cm/2-inch squares

8 cherry tomatoes

8 baby onions, peeled

marinade
6 tbsp olive oil

3 tbsp dry white wine

1 tsp green peppercorns, crushed

2 tbsp chopped fresh coriander

salt

coriander pesto
55 g/2 oz fresh coriander leaves

15 g/½ oz fresh parsley leaves

1 garlic clove

55 g/2 oz pine kernels

25 g/1 oz Parmesan cheese, grated

6 tbsp extra virgin olive oil

juice of 1 lemon

MAPLE-GLAZED TURKEY BURGERS

SERVES 4

2 sweetcorn cobs (in their husks)

450 g/1 lb fresh turkey mince

1 red pepper, deseeded and finely chopped

6 spring onions, finely chopped

55 g/2 oz fresh white breadcrumbs

2 tbsp chopped fresh basil

1 tbsp sunflower oil

2 tbsp maple syrup

salt and pepper

to serve

rocket leaves

tomato slices

cheese-topped hamburger buns, split

sweetcorn relish

Heat a griddle pan until hot, then add the sweetcorn cobs and cook over a medium–high heat, turning occasionally, for 8–10 minutes, or until the husks are charred. Remove from the griddle pan and leave to cool, then strip off the husks and silks. Using a sharp knife, cut away the kernels and place in a bowl.

Add the turkey mince, red pepper, spring onions, breadcrumbs and basil to the sweetcorn kernels in the bowl. Season to taste with salt and pepper. Mix together, then shape into 4 equal-sized burgers. Cover and leave to chill in the refrigerator for 1 hour.

Preheat the barbecue. Brush the burgers with the oil and maple syrup and cook over medium–hot coals for 5–6 minutes on each side, or until cooked through.

Place the rocket and tomato slices on the bottom halves of the buns and top with the burgers. Spoon over a little relish, add the lids and serve immediately.

SPICY TURKEY & CHORIZO KEBABS

Put the oil, garlic, chilli and salt and pepper to taste in a small screw-top jar, screw the lid on tightly and shake well to combine. Leave to stand for 1 hour for the garlic and chilli to flavour the oil.

Preheat the barbecue. Using a sharp knife, cut the turkey into 2.5-cm/1-inch pieces. Cut the chorizo into 2.5-cm/1-inch lengths. Core the apple and cut into chunks. Sprinkle the apple with the lemon juice to prevent discoloration.

Thread the turkey and chorizo pieces onto 8 metal or pre-soaked wooden skewers, alternating with the apple chunks and bay leaves.

Cook the kebabs over hot coals, turning and basting frequently with the flavoured oil, for 15 minutes, or until the turkey is cooked through.

Transfer the kebabs to warmed serving plates and serve immediately.

SERVES 8

6 tbsp olive oil

2 garlic cloves, crushed

1 fresh red chilli, deseeded and chopped

350 g/12 oz turkey steaks

300 g/10½ oz chorizo sausage

1 eating apple

1 tbsp lemon juice

8 fresh bay leaves

salt and pepper

DUCK LEGS WITH MANGO RELISH

First make the relish. Combine all the ingredients in a serving bowl. Cover with clingfilm and leave to stand at room temperature for 1 hour to allow the flavours to develop.

Preheat the barbecue. Remove excess fat from the duck legs and prick the skin all over with a fork. Put in a colander and pour over a kettleful of boiling water to encourage the subcutaneous fat to flow. Pat dry with kitchen paper. Make 4 slashes in each leg and insert the lime segments, pushing them well in. Combine the honey, lime juice, salt, pepper and oil, mixing well. Brush the glaze all over the duck legs.

Grease the grill rack. Rake the coals into 2 heaps on either side of the barbecue and place a disposable foil drip pan in the middle. Place the duck legs skin-side down on the rack over the drip tray. Cover and cook over medium coals for 5 minutes, then turn and brush with the glaze. Continue to cook for 15 minutes, covered, turning every 5 minutes and brushing with the remaining glaze. Turn skin-side up and cook for a further 2–3 minutes for medium-rare or 4–5 minutes for medium.

Transfer the duck legs to a warmed serving dish. Cover with foil and leave to rest in a warm place for 10 minutes – the meat will continue to cook as it rests. Serve immediately with the relish.

SERVES 4

- 4 duck legs, about 250 g/9 oz each
- 4 very thin slices of lime, quartered
- 4 tbsp honey
- juice of 1 lime
- ½ tsp salt
- ½ tsp pepper
- 2 tsp sesame oil, for greasing

mango relish

- 1 ripe mango, peeled, stoned and finely diced
- juice of 1 lime
- ½ small red onion, finely diced
- ½ –1 fresh red chilli, deseeded and finely diced
- 5-cm/2-inch piece fresh ginger, squeezed in a garlic press
- 6 tbsp chopped fresh coriander
- 1 tsp sugar
- ½ tsp sea salt

GRILLED DUCK BREASTS WITH PLUM SAUCE

SERVES 4

4 boneless duck breasts,
  about 175 g/6 oz each

6 tbsp Chinese plum sauce

2 tbsp hoisin sauce

juice of ½ small orange

salt and pepper

sliced spring onions,
  to garnish

Place the duck breasts skin-side down on a board. Lift the edge of the skin away from the flesh and trim off about 1 cm/½ inch all round. Turn skin-side up and make 3 diagonal slashes in the skin, but not all the way through to the flesh. Season both sides with salt and pepper to taste and place in a single layer in a shallow dish.

Mix together the plum sauce, hoisin sauce and orange juice. Pour this over the duck breasts, turning to coat. Cover with clingfilm and leave to marinate for 30 minutes at room temperature or for at least 2 hours in the refrigerator.

Preheat the barbecue to medium–hot. Remove the duck breasts from the marinade, scraping off and reserving the marinade. Place on the grill skin-side down, and cook over medium–hot coals for 2–3 minutes. Turn skin-side up, brush with the marinade, and cook for 8 minutes, turning and brushing halfway through. Turn skin-side up and cook for a further 2 minutes for medium–rare or 4 minutes for medium.

Transfer the duck breasts to a warmed dish. Cover with foil and leave to rest in a warm place for 10 minutes – the meat will continue to cook as it rests.

Pour the remaining marinade into a small saucepan. Bring to the boil and boil for 1 minute.

Carve the breasts into 1 cm/½ inch diagonal slices, and arrange on serving plates. Pour over the cooked marinade, garnish with spring onions and serve immediately.

DUCK BURGERS WITH APPLE & PLUM RELISH

Peel, core and grate 1 of the apples and place in a large bowl with the minced duck, 1 tablespoon of the plum sauce, the spring onions, garlic, ½–1 teaspoon of the crushed chillies, half the cranberries and salt and pepper to taste. Mix together, then shape into 4 equal-sized burgers. Cover and leave to chill in the refrigerator for 1 hour.

Preheat the barbecue. Place the burgers on a foil-lined grill rack and cook over medium–hot coals for 4–5 minutes on each side, or until cooked through. Keep warm.

Peel, core and slice the remaining apple. Melt the butter in a frying pan. Add the apple slices, sprinkle with the sugar and cook for 3–4 minutes, or until slightly softened and lightly caramelized. Remove the frying pan from the heat.

To make the relish, heat the apple sauce with the remaining plum sauce, crushed chillies and cranberries, stirring occasionally, for 3 minutes.

To serve, spoon the mashed potato onto 4 serving plates, top with the burgers and the apple slices and spoon over a little of the relish. Serve immediately.

SERVES 4

2 eating apples

450 g/1 lb duck breasts, skin and fat removed, minced

3 tbsp Thai plum sauce

6 spring onions, finely chopped

2 garlic cloves, crushed

1–1½ tsp dried crushed chillies

55 g/2 oz dried cranberries

1 tbsp butter

2–3 tsp demerara sugar

150 ml/5 fl oz apple sauce

salt and pepper

mashed potato with chopped spring onion and chilli, to serve

FRUITY DUCK

Preheat the barbecue. Using a sharp knife, cut a long slit in the fleshy side of each duck breast to make a pocket. Divide the apricots and shallots between the pockets and secure with cocktail sticks.

Mix the honey and oil together in a small bowl and brush all over the duck. Sprinkle with the five-spice powder.

Cook the duck over medium–hot coals for 6–8 minutes on each side, until cooked through. Remove and discard the cocktail sticks. Transfer to a large serving plate and serve immediately.

SERVES 4

4 duck breasts

115 g/4 oz ready-to-eat dried apricots

2 shallots, thinly sliced

2 tbsp honey

1 tsp sesame oil

2 tsp Chinese five-spice powder

DUCK KEBABS WITH HOISIN SAUCE

SERVES 4–6

4 duck breasts, about
   675 g/1 lb 8 oz in total

12 thin slices fresh ginger

oil, for greasing

marinade

3 tbsp hoisin sauce

1 tbsp sugar

1 tbsp dry sherry or Chinese
   rice wine

2 tsp soy sauce

½ tsp salt

¼ tsp Chinese five-spice powder

Trim any excess fat and skin from the duck breasts, then cut them into 2.5-cm/1-inch cubes. Place in a shallow dish. Whisk together the marinade ingredients and pour over the duck. Cover with clingfilm and leave to marinate in the refrigerator for at least 4 hours or overnight.

Preheat the barbecue. Thread the duck cubes onto 4–6 metal or pre-soaked wooden skewers, alternating with the ginger slices. Grease the grill rack. Cook the kebabs over medium–hot coals, turning occasionally, for 15–20 minutes, until browned on the outside and still slightly pink in the middle.

Place in a dish, cover with foil and leave to rest in a warm place for 5 minutes – the meat will continue to cook as it rests. Uncover and serve immediately.

FISH & SEAFOOD

SALMON WITH MANGO SALSA

Preheat the barbecue. Rinse the salmon steaks under cold running water, pat dry with kitchen paper and place in a large, shallow, non-metallic dish. Sprinkle with the lime rind and pour over the lime juice. Season to taste with salt and pepper, cover and leave to stand while you make the salsa.

Place the mango flesh in a bowl with the onion. Cut the passion fruit in half and scoop out the seeds and pulp with a teaspoon into the bowl. Tear the basil leaves and add them to the bowl with the lime juice. Season to taste with salt and stir well. Cover with clingfilm and reserve until required.

Cook the salmon steaks over medium–hot coals for 3–4 minutes on each side. Serve immediately with the salsa.

SERVES 4

4 salmon steaks, about 175 g/6 oz each

finely grated rind and juice of 1 lime or ½ lemon

salt and pepper

lemon wedges and passion fruit halves, to garnish

salsa

1 large mango, peeled, stoned and diced

1 red onion, finely chopped

2 passion fruit

2 fresh basil sprigs

2 tbsp lime juice

salt

SALMON BURGERS WITH PINE KERNELS

Cook the potatoes in a saucepan of lightly salted boiling water for 15–20 minutes, or until tender. Drain well, then mash and reserve. Chop the salmon into chunks.

Reserve a few spinach leaves for serving, then blanch the remainder in a saucepan of boiling water for 2 minutes. Drain, squeezing out any excess moisture, then chop.

Place the spinach in a food processor with the salmon, potatoes, pine kernels, 1 tablespoon of the lemon rind, the parsley and salt and pepper to taste and, using the pulse button, blend together. Shape into 4–6 equal-sized burgers, then cover and leave to chill for 1 hour. Coat the burgers in the flour.

Mix the crème fraîche, cucumber and the remaining lemon rind together in a bowl, then cover and leave to chill until required.

Preheat the barbecue. Brush the burgers with the oil and cook over medium-hot coals for 4–6 minutes on each side, or until cooked through.

Place the reserved spinach leaves on the bottom halves of the buns and top with the burgers, then spoon over a little of the crème fraîche mixture. Add the lids and serve immediately with grilled cherry tomatoes.

SERVES 4–6

300 g/10½ oz potatoes,
  cut into chunks

450 g/1 lb fresh salmon fillet,
  skinned

175 g/6 oz spinach leaves

55 g/2 oz pine kernels, toasted

2 tbsp finely grated lemon rind

1 tbsp chopped fresh parsley

2 tbsp wholemeal flour

200 ml/7 fl oz crème fraîche

4-cm/1½-inch piece cucumber,
  peeled and finely chopped

2 tbsp sunflower oil

salt and pepper

to serve

4–6 wholemeal buns, split

grilled cherry tomatoes

SALMON & DILL CAKES WITH AÏOLI

SERVES 8

300 g/10½ oz cooked salmon, flaked

300 g/10½ oz mashed potato

8 tbsp fresh chopped dill, plus extra sprigs to garnish

6 spring onions, some green part included, finely chopped

1 tbsp coarsely grated lemon rind

1 tbsp cornflour

1 tsp salt

½ tsp pepper

2 eggs, lightly beaten

flour, for dusting

oil, for greasing

aïoli

3 large garlic cloves, peeled

1 tsp sea salt

2 egg yolks, at room temperature

250 ml/9 fl oz extra virgin olive oil

2 tbsp lemon juice

In a large bowl, combine the salmon, potato, dill, spring onions and lemon rind, mixing lightly with a fork. Sprinkle with the cornflour, salt and pepper, then stir in the beaten egg. With floured hands, form into 8 patties about 2 cm/¾ inch thick. Place on a tray lined with greaseproof paper and chill in the refrigerator for at least 2 hours.

Preheat the barbecue. To make the aïoli, place the garlic in a mortar with the sea salt and crush with a pestle to make a smooth paste. Transfer to a large bowl. Beat in the egg yolks. Add the oil, a few drops at a time, whisking constantly, until the mixture is thick and smooth. Beat in the lemon juice. Transfer to a serving bowl, cover with clingfilm and set aside.

Grease a grill rack and a hinged wire grill basket. Brush the patties with oil on both sides and arrange in the basket. Cook over medium–hot coals, covered, for 8 minutes, until golden. Turn and cook the other side, covered, for 4–5 minutes, until golden. Serve with the aïoli, garnished with dill sprigs.

TUNA BURGERS WITH MANGO SALSA

Cook the sweet potatoes in a saucepan of lightly salted boiling water for 15–20 minutes, or until tender. Drain well, then mash and place in a food processor. Cut the tuna into chunks and add to the potatoes.

Add the spring onions, courgette, chilli, and mango chutney to the food processor and, using the pulse button, blend together. Shape into 4–6 equal-sized burgers, then cover and leave to chill for 1 hour.

Meanwhile make the salsa. Slice the mango, reserving 8–12 slices for serving. Finely chop the remainder, then mix with the tomatoes, chilli, cucumber, coriander and honey. Mix well, then spoon into a small bowl. Cover and leave for 30 minutes to allow the flavours to develop.

Preheat the barbecue. Brush the burgers lightly with the oil and cook over hot coals for 4–6 minutes on each side, or until piping hot. Serve immediately with the mango salsa, garnished with lettuce leaves and the reserved mango slices.

SERVES 4–6

225 g/8 oz sweet potatoes, chopped

450 g/1 lb tuna steaks

6 spring onions, finely chopped

175 g/6 oz courgette, grated

1 fresh red jalapeño chilli, deseeded and finely chopped

2 tbsp mango chutney

1 tbsp sunflower oil

salt

lettuce leaves, to garnish

mango salsa

1 large ripe mango, peeled and stoned

2 ripe tomatoes, finely chopped

1 fresh red jalapeño chilli, deseeded and finely chopped

4-cm/1½-inch piece cucumber, finely diced

1 tbsp chopped fresh coriander

1–2 tsp clear honey

CHILLI & GINGER TUNA

Put the tuna steaks in a single layer in a shallow dish. Brush on both sides with the oil and rub with salt and pepper to taste.

To make the marinade, put the sugar and water in a small saucepan and bring to the boil. Boil for 7–8 minutes, until syrupy. Add the ginger, chilli, garlic and lime juice, and boil for another minute. Pour into a bowl and leave to cool completely.

Pour the cold marinade over the tuna steaks, turning to coat. Cover with clingfilm and leave to marinate in the refrigerator for 30–60 minutes, turning occasionally.

Grease the grill rack and a hinged wire grill basket. Place the tuna steaks in the basket, reserving the marinade. Cook over hot coals for 2 minutes. Turn and cook the other side for 1 minute. Remove from the basket and keep warm.

Pour the reserved marinade into a small saucepan. Bring to the boil and boil for 2 minutes. Pour into a small jug. Arrange the tuna on serving plates and serve immediately with lime wedges and the hot marinade.

SERVES 4

- 4 tuna steaks, 2 cm/¾ inch thick, about 175 g/6 oz each
- 2 tbsp olive oil, plus extra for greasing
- salt and pepper
- lime wedges, to serve

chilli & ginger marinade

- 100 g/3½ oz soft brown sugar
- 125 ml/4 fl oz water
- 2.5-cm/1-inch piece fresh ginger, thinly shredded
- 1 fresh green chilli, deseeded and finely chopped
- 1 large garlic clove, crushed
- juice of ½ lime

TUNA & VEGETABLE KEBABS

SERVES 4

4 tuna steaks, about
140 g/5 oz each

2 red onions

12 cherry tomatoes

1 red pepper, deseeded and cut
into 2.5-cm/1-inch pieces

1 yellow pepper, deseeded and cut
into 2.5-cm/1-inch pieces

1 courgette, sliced

1 tbsp chopped fresh oregano

4 tbsp olive oil

salt and pepper

lime wedges, to garnish

salad leaves, to serve

Preheat the barbecue. Cut the tuna into 2.5-cm/1-inch chunks.
Peel the onions and cut each onion lengthways into 6 wedges.

Divide the fish and vegetables evenly among 8 metal or pre-
soaked wooden skewers and set aside. Mix the oregano and oil
together in a small bowl. Season to taste with salt and pepper
and lightly brush the kebabs with the oil mixture.

Cook the kebabs over hot coals, turning occasionally, for
10–15 minutes, until cooked through.

Garnish with lime wedges and serve immediately with the
salad leaves.

FISH & SEAFOOD

129

TUNA WITH CHILLI SALSA

Rinse the tuna thoroughly under cold running water and pat dry with kitchen paper, then place in a large, shallow, non-metallic dish. Sprinkle with the lime rind and pour over the lime juice and oil. Season to taste with salt and pepper, cover with clingfilm and leave to marinate in the refrigerator for up to 1 hour.

Preheat the barbecue. To make the salsa, brush the peppers with the oil and cook over hot coals, turning frequently, for 10 minutes, or until the skin is blackened and charred. Remove from the barbecue and leave to cool slightly, then peel off the skins and discard the seeds. Put the peppers into a food processor with the remaining salsa ingredients and process to a smooth paste. Transfer to a bowl and season to taste with salt and pepper.

Cook the tuna over hot coals for 4–5 minutes on each side, until golden. Transfer to serving plates, garnish with coriander sprigs and lettuce leaves and serve immediately with the salsa and crusty bread.

SERVES 4

4 tuna steaks, about
    175 g/6 oz each

grated rind and juice of 1 lime

2 tbsp olive oil

salt and pepper

fresh coriander sprigs and lettuce
    leaves, to garnish

crusty bread, to serve

chilli salsa

2 orange peppers

1 tbsp olive oil

juice of 1 lime

juice of 1 orange

2–3 fresh red chillies, deseeded
    and chopped

pinch of cayenne pepper

salt and pepper

TROUT WITH WATERCRESS SAUCE

Preheat the barbecue. Remove the heads from the trout and make 2 diagonal slashes on each side in the thickest part of the flesh, about 9 cm/3½ inches apart. Brush all over with oil. Stuff the slashes and the body cavity with the parsley, chives and lemon slices. Season to taste with salt and pepper. Oil a hinged wire basket and place the trout in it.

For the sauce, put the watercress, lemon juice, stock, salt and pepper in a food processor. Blend for 2–3 minutes, scraping down the sides of the bowl frequently. Pour into a jug, stir in the cream and yogurt and mix well.

Grease the grill rack. Cook the trout over hot coals for 5–6 minutes on each side, or until cooked through.

Carefully remove the trout from the basket, using the tip of a knife to ease the skin away from the wire. Serve immediately on warmed plates with lemon wedges and the watercress sauce.

SERVES 4

4 whole trout, about 350 g/12 oz each, cleaned

olive oil, for greasing

1 small bunch fresh flat-leaf parsley

1 small bunch fresh chives

1 lemon, thinly sliced

salt and pepper

lemon wedges, to serve

watercress sauce

2 bunches watercress, coarse stalks discarded, roughly chopped

juice of ½ lemon

3 tbsp vegetable or fish stock

¼ tsp salt

¼ tsp pepper

4 tbsp double cream

4 tbsp Greek yogurt

SMOKY TROUT BURGERS WITH PESTO RELISH

SERVES 4

225 g/8 oz potatoes

350 g/12 oz smoked trout fillets

2 tsp creamed horseradish

6 spring onions, finely chopped

175 g/6 oz courgette,
roughly grated

2 tbsp wholemeal flour

8 lean back bacon rashers

2 tbsp sunflower oil

salt and pepper

pesto relish

3 tbsp chopped fresh basil

40 g/1½ oz pine kernels, toasted

3 garlic cloves

150 ml/5 fl oz virgin olive oil

40 g/1½ oz Parmesan cheese,
grated

4-cm/1½-inch piece cucumber,
peeled and finely diced

4 spring onions, finely chopped

2 plum tomatoes, finely diced

to serve

chargrilled red pepper strips

hamburger buns, split

Peel the potatoes and cut into chunks. Cook the potatoes in a saucepan of lightly salted water for 15–20 minutes, or until tender. Drain, mash and place in a large bowl. Flake the trout, then add to the bowl with the horseradish, spring onions, courgette and salt and pepper to taste. Mix together and shape into 4 equal-sized burgers. Leave to chill for 1 hour, then coat in the flour and wrap each in 2 rashers of bacon.

Meanwhile, prepare the relish. Place the basil, pine kernels and garlic in a food processor and blend for 1 minute. With the motor running, gradually pour in the olive oil and continue to blend until all the oil has been incorporated. Scrape into a bowl and stir in the cheese, cucumber, spring onions and tomatoes. Spoon into a serving bowl.

Preheat the barbecue. Brush the burgers with the sunflower oil and cook over medium–hot coals for 3–4 minutes on each side, or until cooked through.

Place the pepper strips on the bottom halves of the buns and top with the burgers. Spoon over a little pesto relish, add the lids and serve immediately.

SWORDFISH WITH COCONUT GLAZE

Put the swordfish steaks in a single layer in a shallow dish. Rub with the oil and sea salt.

Put the coconut glaze ingredients in a small saucepan and bring to the boil, stirring. Boil for 12–15 minutes, until reduced by half. Strain, pour into a shallow dish and leave to cool completely.

Pour the glaze over the swordfish, turning to coat and making sure the steaks are completely covered with the glaze. Cover with clingfilm and leave to marinate in the refrigerator for 30–60 minutes.

Preheat the barbecue. Grease the grill rack and a hinged wire grill basket. Drain the swordfish, reserving the marinade. Brush the swordfish with oil on both sides and arrange in the basket. Cook over medium-hot coals, covered, for 5–6 minutes, or until blackened. Turn and cook the other side for 1 minute, or until the flesh is no longer opaque.

Meanwhile, pour the marinade into a small saucepan. Bring to the boil and boil for 3 minutes. Pour into a small jug.

Carefully remove the swordfish from the basket. Arrange in a warmed serving dish, sprinkle with the coriander and serve immediately with the coconut glaze.

SERVES 4

- 4 swordfish steaks, 2 cm/¾ inch thick, about 175 g/6 oz each
- 2 tbsp olive oil, plus extra for greasing
- 1 tsp sea salt
- 1 tbsp chopped fresh coriander, to garnish

coconut glaze
- 425 ml/15 fl oz can coconut cream
- 125 ml/4 fl oz rum
- 4 tbsp soy sauce
- 1 tbsp black peppercorns, cracked
- 5-cm/2-inch piece cinnamon stick, broken

SWORDFISH KEBABS

To make the marinade, whisk the oil, lemon juice, garlic, pepper and paprika together in a non-metallic bowl. Add the swordfish chunks and toss until the swordfish is thoroughly coated. Scatter the onion and torn bay leaves over the top. Cover and leave to marinate in the refrigerator for at least 4 hours.

Meanwhile, make the dressing. Whisk all the ingredients together in a small bowl, cover and set aside.

Put the whole bay leaves in a heatproof bowl, pour over enough boiling water to cover and leave to soften for 1 hour. Drain well and pat dry.

Preheat the barbecue. Drain the swordfish and onion wedges, reserving the marinade. Thread the swordfish onto 4–6 metal or pre-soaked wooden skewers, alternating with the soaked bay leaves and onion wedges. Grease the grill rack. Cook the kebabs over hot coals, turning frequently and basting with the reserved marinade, for 10–15 minutes, until cooked through. Discard the bay leaves before eating and serve the swordfish with the dressing.

SERVES 4–6

600 g/1 lb 5 oz swordfish steaks, 2.5 cm/1 inch thick, cut into 2.5-cm/1-inch chunks

20 fresh bay leaves

olive oil, for oiling

marinade

4 tbsp extra virgin olive oil

2 tbsp lemon juice

1 garlic clove, crushed to a paste with ¼ tsp salt

¼ tsp white pepper

pinch of hot or smoked paprika, to taste

1 onion, cut into wedges

4 fresh bay leaves, torn in half

dressing

5 tbsp extra virgin olive oil

5 tbsp lemon juice

2 tbsp chopped fresh dill

POLENTA COD BURGERS

SERVES 4–6

300 ml/10 fl oz water

225 g/8 oz instant polenta

450 g/1 lb cod fillets, skinned

1 tbsp chopped fresh basil

55 g/2 oz Parmesan cheese, grated

2 tbsp plain flour

1–2 tbsp olive oil

salt and pepper

aïoli

4 garlic cloves, crushed

2 egg yolks

2 tsp lemon juice, plus extra if needed

300 ml/10 fl oz extra virgin olive oil

salt and pepper

to serve

baby spinach leaves

wedges of ciabatta bread

roasted Mediterranean vegetables

Place the water in a large saucepan and bring to the boil. Slowly pour in the polenta in a steady stream and cook over a gentle heat, stirring constantly, for 5 minutes or until thick. Leave to cool for about 10 minutes.

Place the polenta, fish, basil, cheese and salt and pepper to taste in a food processor and, using the pulse button, blend together. Shape into 4–6 burgers, then coat in the flour. Cover and leave to chill in the refrigerator for 1 hour.

Meanwhile, make the aïoli. Place the garlic and egg yolks in a food processor and blend for 1 minute. Add the lemon juice and blend again. With the motor running, slowly pour in the oil until a thick mayonnaise is formed. Add salt and pepper to taste and, if too thick, add a little extra lemon juice.

Preheat the barbecue. Brush the burgers with the oil and cook over medium–hot coals for 4–5 minutes on each side, or until cooked through.

Place the spinach leaves on the ciabatta and top with the burgers, then spoon over a little of the aïoli. Serve immediately with roasted Mediterranean vegetables.

FISH & MANGO KEBABS

Thread the fish, courgette and mango onto 4 metal or pre-soaked wooden skewers and brush lightly with 1 tablespoon of the chilli sauce.

Mix the yogurt, the remaining chilli sauce and the coriander together in a bowl until smooth. Spoon into a serving dish, cover and chill in the refrigerator until required.

Preheat the barbecue. Cook the kebabs over hot coals, turning occasionally, for 10–15 minutes, or until cooked through. Transfer to a serving plate and serve with the yogurt sauce for dipping and lime wedges for squeezing over.

SERVES 4

85 g/3 oz fresh tuna steak, cut into chunks

85 g/3 oz swordfish steak, cut into chunks

1 courgette, cut into chunks

1 ripe mango, peeled, stoned and cut into chunks

2 tbsp sweet chilli sauce

4 tbsp low-fat natural yogurt

1 tbsp chopped fresh coriander

lime wedges, to serve

CARIBBEAN FISH KEBABS

Using a sharp knife, cut the fish into 2.5-cm/1-inch cubes and place in a shallow, non-metallic dish. Place the oil, lime juice, garlic and paprika in a jug and mix well. Season to taste with salt and pepper. Pour the marinade over the fish, turning to coat. Cover with clingfilm and leave to marinate in the refrigerator for 1 hour.

Preheat the barbecue. Drain the fish, reserving the marinade. Thread the fish cubes, onion wedges and tomato wedges alternately onto 6 metal or pre-soaked wooden skewers.

Cook the kebabs over medium–hot coals, turning frequently and brushing with the reserved marinade, for 8–10 minutes, or until cooked through. Transfer to a large plate and serve immediately.

SERVES 6

1 kg/2 lb 4 oz swordfish steaks

3 tbsp olive oil

3 tbsp lime juice

1 garlic clove, finely chopped

1 tsp paprika

3 onions, cut into wedges

6 tomatoes, cut into wedges

salt and pepper

HALIBUT STEAKS WITH SALSA VERDE

SERVES 4

2–3 tbsp olive oil, plus extra for greasing

juice of ½ lemon

¼ tsp sea salt

¼ tsp pepper

4 halibut steaks, 2 cm/¾ inch thick, about 175–225 g/ 6–8 oz each

lemon wedges, to serve

salsa verde

2 anchovy fillets, rinsed and drained

50 g/1¾ oz stale breadcrumbs

25 g/1 oz fresh flat-leaf parsley leaves

25 g/1 oz fresh basil leaves

2 tbsp capers, rinsed

1 garlic clove, crushed

2 tbsp lemon juice

125 ml/4 fl oz olive oil

salt and pepper

To make the marinade, combine the oil, lemon juice, sea salt and pepper in a shallow dish. Add the halibut steaks and turn to coat. Cover with clingfilm and leave to marinate in the refrigerator for 1 hour, turning halfway through.

Preheat the barbecue. Combine all the salsa ingredients in a food processor and briefly pulse 4–5 times to a rough paste. Pour into a bowl and set aside.

Grease the grill rack and a hinged wire grill basket. Place the halibut in the basket, reserving the marinade. Cook over hot coals, brushing with the reserved marinade, for 4–6 minutes on each side, or until golden and cooked through.

Carefully remove the halibut from the basket and place on serving plates. Serve immediately with the salsa verde and lemon wedges for squeezing over.

BARBECUED SNAPPER

Preheat the barbecue. Cut out 4 squares of double-thickness foil, each large enough to hold a whole fish.

Chop the basil leaves. Cream the butter in a bowl with a wooden spoon, then beat in the chopped basil and the garlic.

Season the fish inside and out with salt and pepper to taste. Put a fish on a square of foil. Spoon a quarter of the basil and garlic butter into the cavity and wrap the foil around the fish to enclose it completely. Repeat with the remaining fish.

Put the fish parcels on the grill rack and cook over medium–hot coals for 25–30 minutes, or until cooked through and the fish flakes easily. Transfer to plates and unwrap. Carefully slide out the fish and the cooking juices onto the plates and serve immediately.

SERVES 4

2 bunches fresh basil

85 g/3 oz butter, softened

4 garlic cloves, crushed

4 red snapper or red mullet, about 350 g/12 oz each, scaled, trimmed and cleaned

salt and pepper

ORANGE & LEMON MONKFISH

Cut 8 orange slices and 8 lemon slices, reserving the remaining fruit. Rinse the monkfish fillets under cold running water and pat dry with kitchen paper. Place the monkfish fillets, cut-side up, on a work surface and divide the citrus slices among them. Top with the lemon thyme. Tie each fillet at intervals with kitchen string to secure the citrus slices and thyme. Place the monkfish in a large, shallow, non-metallic dish.

Squeeze the juice from the remaining fruit and mix with the oil in a jug. Season to taste with salt, then spoon the mixture over the fish. Cover with clingfilm and leave to marinate in the refrigerator for up to 1 hour, spooning the marinade over the fish once or twice.

Preheat the barbecue. Drain the monkfish tails, reserving the marinade. Sprinkle the crushed green peppercorns over the fish, pressing them in with your fingers. Cook the monkfish over medium–hot coals, turning and brushing frequently with the reserved marinade, for 20–25 minutes. Transfer to a chopping board, remove and discard the string and cut the monkfish tails into slices. Serve immediately.

SERVES 8

2 oranges

2 lemons

2 monkfish tails, about
   500 g/1 lb 2 oz each, skinned
   and cut into 4 fillets

8 fresh lemon thyme sprigs

2 tbsp olive oil

2 tbsp green peppercorns,
   lightly crushed

salt

MONKFISH & PRAWN KEBABS

SERVES 4

600 g/1 lb 5 oz monkfish fillets

1 green pepper

1 onion

3 tbsp olive oil, plus extra for greasing

3 tbsp lemon juice

2 garlic cloves, crushed

16 large raw prawns, peeled and deveined

16 fresh bay leaves

salt and pepper

Cut the monkfish into 2.5-cm/1-inch chunks. Cut the pepper into similar sized chunks, discarding the core and seeds. Cut the onion into 6 wedges then cut each wedge in half widthways and separate the layers.

To make the marinade, put the oil, lemon juice, garlic, and salt and pepper to taste in a bowl and whisk together. Add the monkfish, prawns, onion, green pepper and bay leaves and toss together until coated in the marinade. Cover and leave to marinate in the refrigerator for 2–3 hours.

Preheat the barbecue. Drain the monkfish, prawns, green pepper, onion and bay leaves, reserving the marinade, then thread alternately onto 8 metal or pre-soaked wooden skewers.

Grease the grill rack. Cook the kebabs over hot coals, turning frequently and brushing with the reserved marinade, for 10–15 minutes, until cooked through. Discard the bay leaves before eating and serve the kebabs immediately.

PRAWNS WITH CITRUS SALSA

Preheat the barbecue. To make the salsa, peel the orange and cut into segments. Reserve any juice. Put the orange segments, apple quarters, chillies, garlic, coriander and mint into a food processor and process until smooth. With the motor running, add the lime juice through the feeder tube. Transfer the salsa to a serving bowl with salt and pepper to taste. Cover with clingfilm and leave to chill in the refrigerator until required.

Using a sharp knife, remove and discard the heads from the prawns, then peel off the shells. Cut along the back of the prawns and remove the dark intestinal vein. Rinse the prawns under cold running water and pat dry with kitchen paper. Mix the chopped coriander, cayenne and sunflower oil together in a dish. Add the prawns and toss well to coat.

Cook the prawns over medium-hot coals for 3 minutes on each side, or until they have changed colour. Transfer to a large serving plate, garnish with coriander leaves and serve immediately with the salsa and lemon wedges for squeezing over.

SERVES 6

36 large raw prawns

2 tbsp finely chopped fresh coriander, plus extra leaves to garnish

pinch of cayenne pepper

3–4 tbsp sunflower oil

lemon wedges, to serve

salsa

1 orange

1 tart eating apple, peeled, quartered and cored

2 fresh red chillies, deseeded and chopped

1 garlic clove, chopped

8 fresh coriander sprigs

8 fresh mint sprigs

4 tbsp lime juice

salt and pepper

PRAWN & SCALLOP KEBABS

Using a sharp knife, remove and discard the heads from the prawns, then remove the shells but leave the tails attached. Cut along the back of the prawns and remove the dark intestinal vein. Remove the tough muscle from the side of the scallops. Slice in half lengthways through the coral.

Combine the oil and lime juice in a shallow dish. Season to taste with salt and pepper. Add the scallops and prawns, and leave to marinate for 15 minutes.

Preheat the barbecue. Drain the prawns and scallops, reserving the marinade. Thread the prawns and scallops alternately onto 8 metal or pre-soaked wooden skewers.

Grease the grill rack. Cook the kebabs over hot coals, turning frequently and brushing with the reserved marinade, for 4–6 minutes, or until cooked through and the prawns have changed colour. Arrange on a serving plate, sprinkle with the coriander and serve immediately with lime wedges for squeezing over.

SERVES 4

24 raw tiger prawns

12 large scallops, corals attached

4–5 tbsp olive oil, plus extra for greasing

juice of 1 lime

1 tbsp chopped fresh coriander

salt and pepper

lime wedges, to serve

SQUID WITH LEMON-GARLIC BUTTER

SERVES 4

6 squid

1–2 fresh red chillies, deseeded and very finely chopped

2 tbsp lemon juice

sunflower oil, for greasing

salt and pepper

rocket leaves, to serve

snipped fresh chives, to garnish

lemon-garlic butter

3 large garlic cloves, thinly sliced

55 g/2 oz butter

juice of 2 lemons

salt and pepper

Preheat the barbecue. Cut open the squid and spread out the body to make a flat piece. Scrape out the guts and remove the eyes and mouth. Reserve the tentacles. Using a serrated knife, score the inner side of the body with a diamond pattern. Mix the chillies and lemon juice in a bowl with salt and pepper to taste. Add the squid body and tentacles, turning to coat.

To make the lemon-garlic butter, gently fry the garlic in 15 g/½ oz of the butter until just coloured. Add the remaining butter and the lemon juice. Stir until the butter has melted, with salt and pepper to taste. Pour into a jug and keep warm.

Grease the grill rack. Drain the squid, reserving the marinade. Place the tentacles and body, scored-side down, on the rack. Cook over hot coals for 1 minute, then turn, brush with the marinade and cook for a further minute, until just opaque. Be careful not to overcook.

To serve, arrange some rocket leaves on serving plates. Place the squid on top, garnish with chives and serve immediately with the lemon-garlic butter.

CHARGRILLED DEVILS

Preheat the barbecue. Open the oysters, catching the juice from the shells in a bowl. Cut the oysters from the bottom shells, reserve and tip any remaining juice into the bowl. To make the sauce, add the red chilli, garlic, shallot, parsley and lemon juice to the bowl, with salt and pepper to taste and mix well. Cover the bowl with clingfilm and leave to chill in the refrigerator until required.

Cut each bacon rasher in half across the centre. Season the oysters with the paprika and cayenne, then roll each oyster up inside half a bacon rasher. Thread the wrapped oysters onto 6 metal or pre-soaked wooden skewers.

Cook over hot coals, turning frequently, for 5 minutes, or until the bacon is well browned and crispy. Transfer to a large serving plate and serve immediately with the sauce.

SERVES 6

36 fresh oysters

18 streaky bacon rashers, rinded

1 tbsp mild paprika

1 tsp cayenne pepper

sauce

1 fresh red chilli, deseeded and finely chopped

1 garlic clove, finely chopped

1 shallot, finely chopped

2 tbsp finely chopped fresh parsley

2 tbsp lemon juice

salt and pepper

THAI CRAB
CAKES

Put the crabmeat, coriander, eggs, cornflour, fish sauce and curry paste in a food processor. Process to a smooth paste. Tip into a bowl, stir in the spring onions and chilli, and season to taste with pepper.

With floured hands, form into 8 patties about 2 cm/¾ inch thick. Place on a tray lined with greaseproof paper and chill in the refrigerator for at least 2 hours.

Preheat the barbecue. Grease the grill rack and a hinged wire grill basket. Brush the patties with oil on both sides and arrange in the basket. Cook over medium–hot coals, covered, for 8 minutes, until golden. Turn and cook the other side for 4–5 minutes.

Carefully remove the cakes from the basket, using the tip of a small knife to separate them from the wire. Arrange in a warmed serving dish and serve immediately with sweet chilli sauce and soured cream.

SERVES 4

450 g/1 lb cooked white crabmeat

6 tbsp chopped fresh coriander

2 eggs, lightly beaten

1 tbsp cornflour

1 tsp Thai fish sauce

1 tsp Thai green curry paste

4 spring onions, finely chopped

1 fresh green chilli, deseeded and finely chopped

vegetable oil, for greasing

flour, for dusting

pepper

sweet chilli sauce and soured cream, to serve

LOBSTER WITH LEMON & CHIVES

SERVES 4

2 live lobsters, about
550 g/1 lb 4 oz each

75 g/2¾ oz unsalted butter,
melted

juice of ½ lemon

2 tsp snipped fresh chives

salt and pepper

small bunch of watercress,
to garnish

lemon wedges and crusty bread,
to serve

Immediately after purchase, put the lobsters in the freezer
at −20°C/−4°F for at least 30 minutes or up to 2 hours.

Preheat the barbecue. Remove the lobsters from the freezer.
Flatten out the tail and grasp with 1 hand at the point where the
tail joins the body. To kill the lobster instantly, take a wide-bladed
pointed knife in the other hand and plunge it into the centre of
the lobster's head, moving the blade towards the eyes. Slice
the lobsters in half lengthways through the head, back and tail.
Remove and discard the gills, the round whitish stomach sac near
the head, and the long intestinal vein running down the side of
the tail. The green tomally, or liver, is considered a delicacy. Cut
off the claws and lightly crack with a hammer.

Brush the lobster flesh with a little of the melted butter and
season to taste with salt and pepper. Place the claws on the grill
rack and cook over hot coals for 2 minutes. Turn and cook for a
further 2 minutes, leaving them on the rack. Place the lobster
halves on the rack, cut-side down, and cook for 3 minutes. Turn
and brush the flesh with a little melted butter. Cook for a further
5–10 minutes, brushing with butter occasionally, or until the flesh
becomes white and opaque.

Transfer the lobster to a warmed serving dish. Sprinkle with the
lemon juice, chives, the remaining melted butter and a little more
salt and pepper. Garnish with watercress and serve immediately
with lemon wedges and crusty bread.

VEGETARIAN

THE ULTIMATE VEGETARIAN BURGER

Cook the rice in a saucepan of lightly salted boiling water for 20 minutes, or until tender. Drain and place in a food processor.

Add the beans, cashew nuts, garlic, onion, sweetcorn, tomato purée, oregano and salt and pepper to taste to the rice in the food processor and, using the pulse button, blend together. Shape into 4–6 equal-sized burgers, then coat in the flour. Cover and leave to chill in the refrigerator for 1 hour.

Preheat the barbecue. Brush the burgers with the oil and cook over medium–hot coals for 5–6 minutes on each side, or until cooked through.

Place the shredded lettuce leaves on the bottom halves of the buns and top with the burgers. Top each with 1 or 2 tomato slices and a cheese slice. Place under a hot grill for 2 minutes, until the cheese begins to melt. Add the lids and serve immediately.

SERVES 4–6

85 g/3 oz brown rice

400 g/14 oz canned flageolet beans, drained and rinsed

115 g/4 oz unsalted cashew nuts

3 garlic cloves

1 red onion, cut into wedges

115 g/4 oz sweetcorn kernels

2 tbsp tomato purée

1 tbsp chopped fresh oregano

2 tbsp wholemeal flour

2 tbsp sunflower oil

salt and pepper

to serve

shredded lettuce leaves

4–6 wholemeal buns, split

8–12 tomato slices

4–6 halloumi cheese slices

MUSHROOM, SPINACH & RICE BURGERS

Cook the rice in a saucepan of boiling water for 12–15 minutes, or until tender. Drain and place in a food processor.

Heat 1 tablespoon of the oil in a frying pan. Add the garlic and mushrooms and cook for 5 minutes. Add to the rice in the food processor.

Reserve 25 g/1 oz spinach leaves. Take the remaining spinach and lightly rinse and pat the leaves completely dry with kitchen paper. Place the spinach, beans, pepper, almonds, Parmesan cheese, basil, breadcrumbs and salt and pepper to taste to the rice mixture in the food processor and, using the pulse button, chop finely. Mix well, then shape into 4–6 equal-sized burgers. Coat in the flour, then cover and leave to chill in the refrigerator for 1 hour.

Preheat the barbecue. Brush the burgers with 2 tablespoons of the remaining oil and cook over medium–hot coals for 5–6 minutes on each side, or until cooked through. Meanwhile, brush the tomato slices and mushrooms with the remaining oil and add to the barbecue for the last 3 minutes of cooking to heat through.

Place the reserved spinach leaves on individual serving plates and top each with a mushroom. Add the burgers and tomato slices and serve immediately.

SERVES 4–6

25 g/1 oz mixed basmati and wild rice

4 tbsp olive oil

3–4 garlic cloves, crushed

300 g/10½ oz button mushrooms, chopped

175 g/6 oz fresh spinach leaves

300 g/10½ oz canned borlotti beans, drained

1 orange pepper, deseeded, peeled and finely chopped

55 g/2 oz flaked almonds, toasted

55 g/2 oz Parmesan cheese, grated

2 tbsp chopped fresh basil

55 g/2 oz fresh wholemeal breadcrumbs

2 tbsp wholemeal flour

1–2 beef tomatoes, thickly sliced

4–6 large field mushrooms

salt and pepper

COURGETTES ON GRILLED POLENTA

SERVES 3–4

2 large yellow or green courgettes

3 tbsp olive oil, plus extra for greasing

1 tsp fresh thyme leaves

coarsely grated rind of ½ lemon

salt and pepper

mixed salad, to serve

polenta

1 litre/1¾ pints water

½ tsp salt

200 g/7 oz polenta

Oil a 30 x 20-cm/12 x 8-inch shallow roasting tin. To make the polenta, pour the water and salt into a large, heavy-based saucepan. Bring to the boil. Stirring constantly with a long-handled wooden spoon, gradually add the polenta in a thin stream. Stir for 20–30 minutes until the mixture is very smooth and starts to come away from the sides of the pan. Tip into the prepared roasting tin, spread into the corners and level the surface. Once cool and firm, slice into 12 fingers measuring about 10 x 5 cm/4 x 2 inches. Remove from the tin and brush both sides with oil.

Preheat the barbecue. Trim the ends from the courgettes. Slice the courgettes lengthways into 1 cm/½ inch thick strips. Carefully peel some of the skin from the outer strips to expose the flesh. Slice the strips in half crossways and place in a shallow dish. Sprinkle with the oil, thyme, lemon rind and salt and pepper to taste, turning to coat. Leave to marinate at room temperature for 30 minutes.

Grease the grill rack. Cook the polenta fingers for 5–6 minutes each side, until slightly charred. Remove and keep warm.

Drain the courgette slices, reserving the marinade. Cook the courgettes over medium–hot coals for 1½–2 minutes. Turn, brush with the reserved marinade and cook for a further 1–1½ minutes, until slightly charred. Place the courgettes on the polenta fingers, and serve immediately with mixed salad.

MUSHROOM & HALLOUMI KEBABS

To make the marinade, mix the lemon rind and juice, oil, thyme and chilli together in a small bowl with salt and pepper to taste.

Place the shiitake and button mushrooms in a large bowl. Cut the halloumi cheese into 2.5-cm/1-inch cubes and add to the mushrooms. Pour over the marinade and toss gently to coat evenly. Cover with clingfilm and leave to marinate in the refrigerator for 2 hours.

Preheat the barbecue. Thread the marinated mushrooms and halloumi cheese onto metal or pre-soaked wooden skewers, reserving any remaining marinade for basting.

Cook the kebabs over medium–hot coals, turning and basting frequently with the marinade, for 10 minutes. Serve immediately.

SERVES 4

16 fresh shiitake mushrooms, about 115 g/4 oz

16 button mushrooms, about 225 g/8 oz

350 g/12 oz halloumi cheese

marinade

grated rind and juice of 2 small lemons

2 tbsp olive oil

2 tbsp chopped fresh thyme

1 small fresh red chilli, deseeded and finely chopped

salt and pepper

YAM & RED PEPPER BURGERS

Cook the yam in a saucepan of lightly salted boiling water for 15–20 minutes, or until tender. Drain well and place in a food processor.

Add the chickpeas, red peppers, garlic, olives, sesame seeds, coriander, and salt and pepper to taste to the yam in the food processor and, using the pulse button, blend together. Shape into 4–6 equal-sized burgers, then coat in the flour. Cover and leave to chill in the refrigerator for 1 hour.

Preheat the barbecue. Brush the burgers with the oil and cook over medium coals for 5–6 minutes on each side, or until cooked through.

Place the rocket leaves on the bottom halves of the buns and top with the burgers. Top with a little hummus and tomato salsa. Add the lids and serve immediately.

SERVES 4–6

225 g/8 oz yam, peeled and cut into chunks

400 g/14 oz canned chickpeas, drained

2 red peppers, deseeded and chopped

2–3 garlic cloves, crushed

85 g/3 oz stoned black olives

2 tbsp sesame seeds

1 tbsp chopped fresh coriander

2 tbsp wholemeal flour

2 tbsp sunflower oil

salt and pepper

to serve

rocket leaves

cheese-topped hamburger buns, split

hummus

tomato salsa

MIXED VEGETABLE BRUSCHETTA

SERVES 4

olive oil, for greasing and drizzling

1 large red pepper, halved and deseeded

1 large orange pepper, halved and deseeded

4 thick slices baguette or ciabatta

1 fennel bulb, sliced

1 red onion, sliced

2 courgettes, sliced diagonally

2 garlic cloves, halved

1 tomato, halved

salt and pepper

Preheat the barbecue. Grease the grill rack. Cut each pepper half lengthways into 4 strips. Toast the bread on both sides in a toaster or under a grill.

Cook the pepper strips and fennel over medium–hot coals for 4 minutes, then add the onion and courgettes and cook for a further 5 minutes, until all the vegetables are tender but still with a slight 'bite'.

Meanwhile, rub the garlic halves over the toasted bread, then rub with the tomato halves. Place on warmed plates. Pile the chargrilled vegetables on top, drizzle with oil and season to taste with salt and pepper. Serve immediately.

VEGETABLE KEBABS WITH BLUE CHEESE

Trim the leeks to about 15 cm/6 inches long. Slice in half lengthways and then crossways into 2.5-cm/1-inch pieces.

Thread the leeks, tomatoes and mushrooms alternately onto 12 metal or pre-soaked wooden skewers. Brush with the melted butter and season to taste with salt and pepper.

Grease the grill rack. Cook the kebabs over medium–hot coals, turning frequently, for 6–10 minutes, or until thoroughly cooked. Transfer to a plate, sprinkle with the cheese and serve immediately.

SERVES 6

5 thin leeks

18 cherry tomatoes, halved

24 chestnut mushrooms

100 g/3½ oz butter, melted

125 g/4½ oz blue cheese, crumbled

oil, for greasing

salt and pepper

POTATO KEBABS
WITH FETA

Preheat the barbecue. Using a mortar and pestle, crush the garlic cloves with the sea salt until smooth and creamy. Add the rosemary and pepper, and pound to a paste. Whisk in the oil, then pour the mixture into a large bowl and leave to stand.

Scrub the potatoes and slice in half crossways. Steam over boiling water for 7 minutes, or until just tender. Spread out on a clean tea towel to dry. Add to the garlic mixture in the bowl and toss to coat.

Arrange the potatoes cut-side down on a board, reserving the remaining garlic mixture. Thread onto 6 metal or pre-soaked wooden skewers, piercing the potato halves through the middle so that the cut sides remain facing downwards.

Heap some of the coals to one side, leaving a slightly cooler area with a single layer of coals. Grease a grill rack. Cook the kebabs over hot coals, cut-side down, for 3–4 minutes. Brush with the garlic mixture, then turn and move to the cooler area. Cook for a further 5–7 minutes, until tender when pierced with the tip of a knife.

Arrange the kebabs on a serving plate and sprinkle with the feta and parsley. Serve immediately.

SERVES 6

4 large garlic cloves, peeled

1 tsp sea salt

1 tbsp finely chopped fresh rosemary

½ tsp pepper

4 tbsp olive oil, plus extra for greasing

850 g/1 lb 14 oz salad potatoes

40 g/1½ oz crumbled feta cheese

1 tbsp chopped fresh flat-leaf parsley

HALLOUMI & RED PEPPER SANDWICHES

SERVES 4

1 small red pepper, quartered lengthways and deseeded

olive oil, for greasing

250 g/9 oz halloumi cheese

small handful fresh oregano leaves, chopped

salt and pepper

Preheat the barbecue. Brush the pepper quarters with oil and arrange in a hinged wire grill basket. Cook for 8–10 minutes, turning once, until slightly charred. Remove the skin and slice the flesh crossways into thin strips.

Slice the halloumi horizontally into 8 rectangles and brush both sides with oil. Arrange the sliced pepper and oregano on 4 of the slices. Season to taste with salt and pepper. Make into sandwiches by topping with the remaining 4 halloumi slices.

Place the sandwiches in a hinged wire grill basket. Cook over medium–hot coals for 45–60 seconds, turning when the cheese is speckled with brown. Turn and cook the other side for 45 seconds. Serve immediately.

MUSHROOM CIABATTA BURGERS

Preheat the barbecue. Wipe the mushrooms, but do not peel. Put in a dish with the pepper quarters. Whisk together the oil and garlic, and pour over the vegetables. Season to taste with salt and pepper.

Slice the ciabatta into 8 x 2 cm/¾ inch thick slices about the same size as the mushrooms. Brush with oil.

Grease the grill rack. Cook the mushrooms and peppers over medium–hot coals, covered, for 4–5 minutes on each side, or until slightly charred. Remove from the grill and keep warm.

Toast the ciabatta over medium–low coals for 1–2 minutes on each side, until golden. Place 4 of the ciabatta slices on a board. Place a piece of pepper on top, followed by a mushroom and another piece of pepper. Top with a few rocket leaves, season to taste with salt and pepper and top with the second slice of ciabatta. Serve immediately.

SERVES 4

4 large field mushrooms, stalks trimmed

2 red peppers, quartered lengthways and deseeded

6 tbsp extra virgin olive oil, plus extra for greasing

1 large garlic clove, crushed

1 ciabatta loaf

handful of rocket leaves

salt and pepper

VEGETARIAN SAUSAGES

Heat the oil in a saucepan. Add the onion, mushrooms and pepper and fry until softened.

Mash the beans in a large bowl. Add the onion, mushroom and pepper mixture, the breadcrumbs, cheese, herbs and egg yolk and mix well. Press the mixture together with your fingers and shape into 8 sausages. Roll each sausage in the flour. Leave to chill in the refrigerator for at least 30 minutes.

Preheat the barbecue. Cook the sausages on a sheet of oiled foil set over medium–hot coals, turning and basting frequently with oil, for 15–20 minutes, or until golden.

Split the hot dog rolls down the centre and insert a layer of fried onions and some salad leaves. Place the sausages in the rolls and serve immediately with ketchup.

SERVES 8

1 tbsp sunflower oil,
   plus extra for greasing

1 small onion, finely chopped

50 g/1¾ oz mushrooms,
   finely chopped

½ red pepper, deseeded and finely
   chopped

400 g/14 oz canned cannellini
   beans, rinsed and drained

100 g/3½ oz fresh breadcrumbs

100 g/3½ oz Cheddar cheese,
   grated

1 tsp dried mixed herbs

1 egg yolk

2 tbsp plain flour

to serve
hot dog rolls

fried onions

salad leaves

tomato ketchup

AUBERGINE & MOZZARELLA SANDWICHES

SERVES 2

1 large aubergine

1 tbsp lemon juice

3 tbsp olive oil

125 g/4½ oz mozzarella cheese, grated

2 sun-dried tomatoes, chopped

salt and pepper

to serve
Italian bread

mixed salad leaves

tomato slices

Preheat the barbecue. Using a sharp knife, slice the aubergine into thin rounds.

Mix the lemon juice and oil together in a small bowl and season to taste with salt and pepper. Brush the aubergine slices with the oil and lemon juice mixture and cook over medium–hot coals for 2–3 minutes, without turning, until golden on the under side.

Turn half of the aubergine slices over and sprinkle with the cheese and sun-dried tomatoes.

Place the remaining aubergine slices on top of the cheese and tomatoes, turning them so that the uncooked side is uppermost. Barbecue for 1–2 minutes, then carefully turn the whole sandwich over and barbecue for a further 1–2 minutes.

Serve immediately in Italian bread with mixed salad leaves and tomato slices.

GREEK VEGETABLE KEBABS

Preheat the barbecue. Cut the onions into wedges, then place the onions and potatoes in a saucepan of lightly salted boiling water and cook for 20 minutes, or until just tender. Drain and leave to cool. Meanwhile, blanch the aubergine in boiling water for 2 minutes, then add the cucumber and simmer for 1 minute. Add the peppers and simmer for a further 2 minutes, then drain and leave the vegetables to cool.

Place the cooled vegetables, cheese, nectarines and mushrooms in a bowl. Add the oil and herbs and toss to coat. Thread the vegetables, cheese, nectarines and mushrooms alternately onto 8 metal or pre-soaked wooden skewers.

Cook the kebabs over hot coals, turning frequently, for 15 minutes. Transfer to a large serving plate and serve immediately.

SERVES 4

2 onions

8 new potatoes, halved

1 aubergine, cut into chunks

½ small cucumber, thickly sliced

1 red pepper, deseeded and cut into chunks

1 yellow pepper, deseeded and cut into chunks

225 g/8 oz halloumi cheese, cut into cubes

2 nectarines, stoned and cut into wedges

8 button mushrooms

2 tbsp olive oil

2 tsp chopped fresh thyme

2 tsp chopped fresh rosemary

salt

STUFFED MUSHROOMS

Preheat the barbecue. Remove the stalks from the mushrooms and chop the stalks finely. Heat half the oil in a large frying pan. Add the mushroom stalks and spring onions and sauté briefly.

Transfer the mushroom stalks and spring onions to a large bowl. Add the breadcrumbs, oregano and feta cheese and mix well.

Spoon the stuffing mixture into the mushroom caps. Drizzle the remaining oil over the stuffed mushrooms, then cook over medium–hot coals for 8–10 minutes. Transfer the mushrooms to individual serving plates and serve immediately.

SERVES 12

12 large field mushrooms

4 tsp olive oil

4 spring onions, chopped

100 g/3½ oz fresh wholemeal breadcrumbs

1 tsp chopped fresh oregano

100 g/3½ oz feta cheese, crumbled

BAKED SWEET POTATOES WITH CHILLI SALSA

SERVES 4

4 sweet potatoes, about 350 g/
   12 oz each

large knob of butter

2 tbsp chopped fresh coriander

100 g/3½ oz feta cheese,
   crumbled

salt and pepper

salsa

3 tomatoes, deseeded and finely
   diced

1 small red onion, finely diced

½ –1 small fresh green chilli,
   deseeded and finely diced

3 tbsp chopped fresh coriander

juice of 1 lime

salt

Preheat the barbecue. Prick the potatoes all over with a fork
and wrap in foil. Cook over medium–hot coals for 45–55 minutes,
or until tender when pierced with a skewer.

Meanwhile, combine the salsa ingredients in a serving bowl.
Leave to stand at room temperature to let the flavours develop.

Unwrap the potatoes and slice in half. Fork the flesh and mix
in the butter and most of the coriander. Sprinkle with the cheese
and the remaining coriander. Season to taste with salt and
pepper. Serve immediately with the salsa.

YAKITORI VEGETABLE KEBABS

Preheat the barbecue. Thread the vegetables alternately onto 4 metal or pre-soaked wooden skewers.

Mix together the yakitori sauce ingredients and drizzle over the kebabs. Cook the kebabs over medium–hot coals for 10–12 minutes, until the vegetables are just tender but not soft. Serve immediately.

SERVES 4

1 large courgette, sliced

4 spring onions, sliced diagonally

1 orange pepper, deseeded and cubed

100 g/3½ oz button mushrooms, wiped clean

8 cherry tomatoes

yakitori sauce

1 tbsp soy sauce

1 tbsp honey

1 tbsp rice vinegar

BLUE CHEESE & APPLE BURGERS

Cook the potatoes in a saucepan of boiling water for 15–20 minutes, or until tender. Drain and, using a potato masher, crush into small pieces. Place in a large bowl.

Place the nuts and onion in a food processor and, using the pulse button, chop finely. Add the nuts, onion, apple, cheese and breadcrumbs to the potatoes in the bowl. Season to taste with salt and pepper. Mix well, then shape into 4–6 equal-sized burgers. Coat in the flour, then cover and leave to chill in the refrigerator for 1 hour.

Preheat the barbecue. Brush the burgers with the oil and cook over medium coals for 5–6 minutes on each side, or until cooked through.

Place the salad leaves on the bottom halves of the buns and top with the burgers. Top with red onion slices, add the lids and serve immediately.

SERVES 4–6

175 g/6 oz new potatoes

225 g/8 oz mixed nuts, such as pecans, almonds and hazelnuts

1 onion, roughly chopped

2 small eating apples, peeled, cored and grated

175 g/6 oz blue cheese, such as Stilton, crumbled

55 g/2 oz fresh wholemeal breadcrumbs

2 tbsp wholemeal flour

1–2 tbsp sunflower oil

salt and pepper

to serve
salad leaves

cheese-topped hamburger buns, split

red onion slices

BAKED CAMEMBERT

SERVES 4

1 whole Camembert cheese
(about 200 g/7 oz)

2 cloves garlic, thinly sliced

2 sprigs rosemary, cut into small
pieces

4 tbsp white wine (optional)

salt and pepper

crusty French bread, to serve

Preheat the barbecue. Remove the Camembert from its wrapper and place on a piece of double-thickness foil.

Make about 8–10 small incisions in the surface of the cheese using the tip of a small sharp knife.

Push the garlic slices and rosemary sprigs into the incisions and then drizzle over the wine, if using. Season to taste with salt and pepper.

Loosely seal the foil and then cook over low–medium coals for about 10–15 minutes, depending on the heat levels, until the cheese has become soft and molten in the centre. Serve immediately with crusty French bread.

VEGETARIAN

203

MARINATED TOFU SKEWERS

To make the marinade, mix the lemon rind and juice, garlic, rosemary, thyme and walnut oil together in a shallow dish. Drain the tofu, pat it dry on kitchen paper and cut it into squares. Add to the marinade and toss to coat. Leave to marinate for 20–30 minutes.

Preheat the barbecue. Deseed the peppers and cut into 2.5-cm/1-inch pieces. Blanch in boiling water for 4 minutes, refresh in cold water and drain. Using a canelle knife or potato peeler, remove strips of peel from the courgettes. Cut the courgettes into 2.5-cm/1-inch chunks.

Drain the tofu, reserving the marinade. Thread the tofu onto 8 metal or pre-soaked wooden skewers, alternating with the peppers, courgette and button mushrooms.

Cook the skewers over medium-hot coals for 6 minutes, turning and basting with the marinade. Transfer the skewers to warmed serving plates, garnish with shredded carrot and lemon wedges and serve immediately.

SERVES 4

350 g/12 oz firm tofu

1 red pepper

1 yellow pepper

2 courgettes

24 button mushrooms

marinade
grated rind and juice of ½ lemon

1 garlic clove, crushed

½ tsp chopped fresh rosemary

½ tsp chopped fresh thyme

1 tbsp walnut oil

to garnish
shredded carrot

lemon wedges

CHARGRILLED VEGETABLES

Cook the sweet potato slices in boiling water for 5 minutes. Drain and set aside to cool. Sprinkle the courgettes with salt and set aside for 30 minutes. Rinse and pat dry with kitchen paper.

Meanwhile, make the salsa verde. Put the chillies, spring onions and garlic in a food processor and process briefly. Add the capers and parsley, and pulse until finely chopped. Transfer the mixture to a serving bowl. Stir in the lime rind and juice, lemon juice, oil and Tabasco. Season to taste with pepper, cover with clingfilm and chill in the refrigerator until required.

Preheat the barbecue. Brush the sweet potatoes, courgettes and red peppers with oil. Cook over medium–hot coals, turning once and brushing with more oil, for 8–10 minutes, until tender and lightly charred. Serve the vegetables immediately with the salsa verde.

SERVES 6

2 sweet potatoes, sliced

3 courgettes, halved lengthways

3 red peppers, deseeded and cut into quarters

olive oil, for greasing

salt

salsa verde

2 fresh green chillies, halved and deseeded

8 spring onions, roughly chopped

2 garlic cloves, roughly chopped

1 tbsp capers

bunch of fresh parsley, roughly chopped

grated rind and juice of 1 lime

4 tbsp lemon juice

6 tbsp olive oil, plus extra for greasing

1 tbsp green Tabasco sauce

pepper

COURGETTE & FETA PARCELS

SERVES 2

2 large courgettes

115 g/4 oz feta cheese,
   cut into strips

1 tbsp olive oil, plus extra for
   greasing

1 tbsp chopped fresh mint

pepper

Preheat the barbecue. Cut out 2 rectangles of foil, each large
enough to enclose a courgette, and brush lightly with oil. Cut a
few slits along the length of each courgette and place them on
the foil rectangles.

Insert strips of feta cheese along the slits in the courgettes,
then drizzle the oil over the top, sprinkle with the mint and
season to taste with pepper. Fold in the sides of the foil
rectangles securely and seal the edges to enclose the cheese-
stuffed courgettes completely.

Cook the courgette parcels in the barbecue embers for
30–40 minutes. Carefully unwrap the parcels and serve
immediately.

GLAZED
VEGETABLE
KEBABS

Preheat the barbecue. Put the yogurt, chutney, garlic and lemon juice in a bowl with salt and pepper to taste and stir together.

Put the onions in a saucepan of boiling water. Return to the boil, then drain well.

Thread the onions, baby corn, courgettes, mushrooms and tomatoes alternately onto 8 metal or pre-soaked wooden skewers.

Brush the kebabs with the yogurt glaze, then cook over medium–hot coals, turning and brushing frequently, for 10 minutes, until golden and tender.

Serve immediately, garnished with salad leaves.

SERVES 4

150 ml/5 fl oz low-fat natural yogurt

4 tbsp mango chutney

1 tsp chopped garlic

1 tbsp lemon juice

8 baby onions, peeled

8 baby corn, halved

2 courgettes, cut into 2.5-cm/1-inch pieces

16 button mushrooms

8 cherry tomatoes

salt and pepper

salad leaves, to garnish

TOMATO &
MOZZARELLA
STACKS

SERVES 4

4 large tomatoes

225 g/8 oz buffalo mozzarella
cheese

24 basil leaves, plus 4 small
sprigs

olive oil, for greasing

salt and pepper

Preheat the barbecue. Using a sharp serrated knife, cut a thin slice from the top and bottom of each tomato and discard. Cut the rest of the tomato horizontally into 3 slices. Cut the mozzarella into 12 thin rounds. Slice the basil leaves into thin ribbons.

Brush the centre of an 18-cm/7-inch square of foil with oil. Place a tomato slice on the foil, brush with oil and season to taste with salt and pepper. Add a few basil shreds and a slice of cheese. Continue layering using the second and third tomato slices, seasoning each layer with salt and pepper to taste, and finishing with a layer of mozzarella. Add a basil sprig, then fold up the edges of the foil to enclose completely. Repeat with the remaining tomatoes, basil and mozzarella.

Arrange on the grill rack, cook over medium–hot coals, covered, for 8–10 minutes, or until the top tomato slice is heated through and the mozzarella has melted. Open the foil parcels and serve immediately.

SWEET POTATO & HALLOUMI BURGERS

SERVES 4–6

450 g/1 lb sweet potatoes,
  cut into chunks

175 g/6 oz broccoli florets

2–3 garlic cloves, crushed

1 red onion, finely chopped or
  grated

1½–2 fresh red jalapeño chillies,
  deseeded and finely chopped

175 g/6 oz halloumi cheese,
  grated

2 tbsp wholemeal flour

2–3 tbsp sunflower oil

450 g/1 lb onions, sliced

1 tbsp chopped fresh coriander

salt and pepper

to serve

salad leaves

wholemeal buns, split

Cook the sweet potato in a saucepan of lightly salted boiling water for 15–20 minutes, or until tender. Drain and mash. Cut the broccoli into small pieces, cook in a separate saucepan of boiling water for 3 minutes, then drain and plunge into cold water. Drain again, then add to the mashed sweet potato.

Stir in the garlic, onion, chilli, cheese and salt and pepper to taste. Mix well and shape into 4–6 equal-sized burgers, then coat in the flour. Cover and leave to chill in the refrigerator for at least 1 hour.

Heat 1½ tablespoons of the oil in a heavy-based frying pan. Add the onions and fry over a medium heat for 12–15 minutes, or until softened. Stir in the coriander and reserve.

Preheat the barbecue. Brush the burgers with the remaining oil and cook over medium coals for 5–6 minutes on each side, or until cooked through.

Place the salad leaves on the bottom halves of the buns and top with the burgers. Top with the reserved fried onions and coriander, add the lids and serve immediately.

SIDES & SALADS

SUMMER VEGETABLE PARCELS

Preheat the barbecue. Cut out 4 x 30-cm/12-inch squares of foil and divide the vegetables equally among them.

Put the lemon rind, butter, herbs and garlic into a food processor and process until blended, then season to taste with salt and pepper. Alternatively, beat together in a bowl until blended.

Divide the butter equally among the vegetable parcels, dotting it on top. Fold up the sides of the foil to enclose the vegetables, sealing securely. Cook over medium-hot coals, turning occasionally, for 25–30 minutes. Open the parcels, sprinkle with the lemon juice and serve immediately.

SERVES 4

1 kg/2 lb 4 oz prepared vegetables, such as carrots, asparagus, baby corn, cherry tomatoes, leeks, courgettes, chillies and baby onions

grated rind and juice of 1 lemon

115 g/4 oz unsalted butter

3 tbsp chopped mixed fresh herbs, such as parsley, thyme, chives and chervil

2 garlic cloves

salt and pepper

ITALIAN VEGETABLE PLATTER

Preheat the barbecue. Slice a thin sliver from the root end of the fennel bulb, keeping the root intact. Pull off and discard the tough outer layers. Slice the bulb vertically into 8-mm/⅜ inch slices, making sure the layers are still attached to the root. Place in a shallow dish, sprinkle with the oil and vinegar, and season to taste with salt and pepper. Toss gently to coat.

Trim a thin sliver from the root end of the chicory, discard the outer leaves and slice in half lengthways. Make 2 or 3 lengthways cuts in the core without cutting through to the leaves. Slice the pepper in half lengthways and remove the core and seeds. Slice each half lengthways into 3 strips. Slice the tomatoes in half. Trim the spring onions, but keep them whole.

Grease the grill rack. Brush the vegetables with oil and cook over hot coals, starting with the fennel and chicory and adding the remaining vegetables in the order listed. Cook the chicory and tomatoes cut-side down. After each type of vegetable has cooked for 2 minutes, check the underside. Once slightly charred, turn them over with tongs. Brush with more oil and season to taste with salt. Sprinkle the tomatoes with the garlic. Cook for a further 1–3 minutes, depending on the vegetable.

As the vegetables become cooked, transfer to a warmed serving dish. Adjust the seasoning, adding salt and pepper if needed, and garnish with parsley. Serve warm or at room temperature.

SERVES 6

- 1 large fennel bulb
- 1 tbsp extra virgin olive oil, plus extra for greasing
- 1 tsp balsamic vinegar or balsamic glaze
- 3 heads chicory
- 1 large yellow or red pepper
- 3 large tomatoes
- 6 spring onions
- 1 garlic clove, finely chopped
- salt and pepper
- chopped fresh flat-leaf parsley, to garnish

PUMPKIN PARCELS WITH CHILLI & LIME

SERVES 4

700 g/1 lb 9 oz pumpkin or squash

2 tbsp sunflower oil

25 g/1 oz butter

½ tsp chilli sauce

grated rind of 1 lime

2 tsp lime juice

Preheat the barbecue. Halve the pumpkin and scoop out the seeds. Rinse the seeds and reserve. Cut the pumpkin into thin wedges and peel.

Heat the oil and butter together in a large saucepan, stirring, until melted. Stir in the chilli sauce, lime rind and juice. Add the pumpkin and seeds to the saucepan and toss to coat on all sides in the flavoured butter.

Divide the mixture among 4 double-thickness sheets of foil. Fold over the foil to enclose the pumpkin mixture completely.

Cook the foil parcels over hot coals for 15–25 minutes, or until the pumpkin is tender. Transfer the foil parcels to warmed serving plates. Open the parcels and serve immediately.

SIDES & SALADS

223

BEETROOT &
THYME PARCELS

Preheat the barbecue. Place 8 beetroot quarters and a thyme
sprig on a large square of foil. Brush the beetroot
with oil and sprinkle with salt and pepper to taste. Wrap in
a loose parcel, sealing the edges well. Repeat with the
remaining beetroot.

Cook the beetroot over medium–hot coals, turning occasionally,
for 30–40 minutes, or until tender. Open the packages and serve
immediately.

SERVES 4

8 small raw beetroot, peeled and
   quartered lengthways

4 fresh thyme sprigs

olive oil, for greasing

salt and pepper

SWEETCORN COBS WITH BLUE CHEESE

Preheat the barbecue. Crumble the Danish Blue cheese and place in a bowl. Beat with a wooden spoon until creamy. Beat in the curd cheese until thoroughly blended. Gradually beat in the yogurt and season to taste with salt and pepper. Cover with clingfilm and leave to chill in a cool place until required.

Fold back the husks on each sweetcorn cob and remove the silks. Smooth the husks back into place. Cut out 6 rectangles of double-thickness foil, each large enough to enclose a sweetcorn cob. Wrap in the foil.

Cook over medium-hot coals for 15–20 minutes, turning frequently. Unwrap, peel back the husks and trim off with a sharp knife. Serve immediately with the blue cheese dressing.

SERVES 6

140 g/5 oz Danish Blue cheese
140 g/5 oz curd cheese
125 ml/4 fl oz Greek yogurt
6 sweetcorn cobs in their husks
salt and pepper

ROASTED BALSAMIC & HONEY ONIONS

SERVES 4

4 red onions, peeled and cut into chunky wedges

4 tsp honey

4 tbsp balsamic vinegar

1 tsp finely chopped fresh thyme

salt and pepper

Preheat the barbecue. Divide the onion wedges between 4 squares of double-thickness foil. Fold up the sides of the foil a little.

Drizzle the honey and balsamic vinegar over the onions, add the thyme and season to taste with salt and pepper.

Loosely seal the parcels and cook over hot coals for 15–20 minutes, or until the onions are tender. Open the packages and serve immediately.

SQUASH WITH WALNUTS, MINT & YOGURT

Preheat the barbecue. Peel and deseed the squash and cut into chunks about 5 cm/2 inches thick. Steam over boiling water for 5–6 minutes, or until barely tender. Tip into a large bowl. Whisk together the oil, vinegar, sea salt and pepper. Pour this over the squash, tossing to coat.

Grease the grill rack. Drain the squash, reserving the oil mixture, and thread onto 4 metal or pre-soaked wooden skewers. Cook over medium–hot coals, turning and brushing with the oil mixture, for 6–7 minutes, until slightly charred.

Remove from the skewers and put in a serving bowl. Sprinkle with the walnuts and mint leaves and drizzle with the yogurt. Serve warm or at room temperature.

SERVES 4

1 large or 2 small butternut squash

6 tbsp olive oil, plus extra for greasing

2 tbsp balsamic vinegar or balsamic glaze

1 tsp sea salt

1 tsp pepper

handful of walnut halves, toasted

small handful of fresh mint leaves

6 tbsp Greek yogurt

CRISPY POTATO SKINS

Preheat the oven to 200°C/400°F/Gas Mark 6. Prick the potatoes with a fork and bake for 1 hour, or until tender. Alternatively, cook in a microwave on high for 12–15 minutes. Cut the potatoes in half and scoop out the flesh, leaving about 5 mm/¼ inch potato flesh lining the skin.

Preheat the barbecue. Brush the insides of the potato with the melted butter.

Place the skins, cut-side down, over medium–hot coals and cook for 10–15 minutes. Turn the potato skins over and barbecue for a further 5 minutes, or until they are crispy. Take care that they do not burn. Season the potato skins with salt and pepper to taste and serve while they are still warm.

If wished, the skins can be filled with a variety of toppings. Barbecue the potato skins as above for 10 minutes, then turn cut-side up and sprinkle with the spring onion, cheese and salami. Barbecue for a further 5 minutes, or until the cheese begins to melt. Serve immediately.

SERVES 4–6

8 small baking potatoes, scrubbed

50 g/1¾ oz butter, melted

salt and pepper

optional topping

6 spring onions, sliced

50 g/1¾ oz Gruyère cheese, grated

50 g/1¾ oz salami, cut into thin strips

ROSEMARY
POTATOES

SERVES 5–6

675 g/1 lb 8 oz potatoes, scrubbed

225 g/8 oz unsalted butter

2 tbsp chopped fresh rosemary leaves

salt and pepper

Preheat the barbecue. Cut the potatoes into 3 mm/⅛ inch thick slices. Plunge into a large bowl of water to wash off the starch. Drain and pat dry with kitchen paper.

Take a very large sheet of foil and smear some of the butter over an area in the middle measuring about 30 x 20 cm/ 12 x 8 inches. Arrange a single layer of potatoes on the greased area. Sprinkle with some of the rosemary, season to taste with salt and pepper and dot generously with butter. Repeat until the potato slices, rosemary and butter are used up – there should be 3 layers. Fold over the foil to make a flat parcel, sealing the edges well. Wrap the parcel in 2 more large pieces of foil, sealing well.

Cook over hot coals, turning occasionally, for 45 minutes, or until the potatoes are tender. Open the parcels and serve immediately.

SIDES & SALADS

CRISPY BACON & SPINACH SALAD

Heat 2 tablespoons of the oil in a large frying pan over a high heat. Add the bacon to the pan and cook for 3–4 minutes, or until crisp. Remove with a slotted spoon, draining carefully, and set aside.

For the croûtons, toss the cubes of bread in the fat remaining in the pan over a high heat for about 4 minutes, or until crisp and golden. Remove the croûtons with a slotted spoon, draining carefully, and set them aside.

Add the remaining oil to the frying pan and heat. Toss the spinach in the oil over a high heat for about 3 minutes, or until it has just wilted. Turn into a serving bowl and sprinkle with the bacon and croûtons. Serve immediately.

SERVES 4

4 tbsp olive oil

4 streaky bacon rashers, diced

1 thick slice of white bread, crusts removed, cut into cubes

450 g/1 lb fresh spinach, torn or shredded

WARM PASTA SALAD

To make the dressing, whisk the oil, vinegar, sugar and mustard together in a jug. Season to taste with salt and pepper and stir in the basil.

Bring a large saucepan of lightly salted water to the boil. Add the pasta, bring back to the boil and cook for 8–10 minutes, until the pasta is tender but still firm to the bite. Drain and transfer to a serving bowl. Add the dressing and toss well.

Add the sun-dried tomatoes, spring onions, rocket and cucumber, season to taste with salt and pepper and toss. Serve warm.

SERVES 4

225 g/8 oz dried farfalle or other pasta shapes

6 pieces of sun-dried tomato in oil, drained and chopped

4 spring onions, chopped

55 g/2 oz rocket leaves

½ cucumber, deseeded and diced

salt and pepper

dressing

4 tbsp olive oil

1 tbsp white wine vinegar

½ tsp caster sugar

1 tsp Dijon mustard

4 fresh basil leaves, finely shredded

salt and pepper

CAESAR SALAD

SERVES 4

1 large egg

2 cos lettuces or 3 Little Gem
   lettuces

6 tbsp olive oil

2 tbsp lemon juice

8 canned anchovy fillets, drained
   and roughly chopped

85 g/3 oz Parmesan cheese
   shavings

salt and pepper

garlic croûtons

4 tbsp olive oil

2 garlic cloves

5 slices of white bread, crusts
   removed, cut into 1-cm/½-inch
   cubes

To make the garlic croûtons, heat the oil in a heavy-based frying pan. Add the garlic and bread and cook, stirring and tossing frequently, for 4–5 minutes, or until the bread is crispy and golden all over. Remove from the frying pan with a slotted spoon and drain on kitchen paper.

Meanwhile, bring a small pan of water to the boil, add the egg to the boiling water and cook for 1 minute, then remove from the saucepan and reserve.

Arrange the lettuce leaves in a serving bowl. Mix the oil and lemon juice together, then season to taste with salt and pepper. Crack the egg into the dressing and whisk to blend. Pour the dressing over the lettuce leaves, toss well, then add the croûtons and anchovies and toss the salad again. Sprinkle with Parmesan cheese shavings and serve immediately.

THREE-BEAN SALAD

Arrange the salad leaves in a bowl and reserve.

Thinly slice the onion, then cut in half to form half moons and put into a bowl.

Thinly slice the radishes, cut the tomatoes in half and peel the beetroot, if necessary, and dice. Add to the onion with the remaining salad ingredients, except the nuts and cheese.

Put all the ingredients for the dressing into a screw-top jar and shake until blended. Pour over the bean mixture, toss lightly, then spoon on top of the salad leaves.

Scatter over the nuts and cheese and serve immediately.

SERVES 4

175 g/6 oz mixed salad leaves, such as spinach, rocket and frisée

1 red onion

85 g/3 oz radishes

175 g/6 oz cherry tomatoes

115 g/4 oz cooked beetroot

280 g/10 oz canned cannellini beans, drained and rinsed

200 g/7 oz canned red kidney beans, drained and rinsed

300 g/10½ oz canned flageolet beans, drained and rinsed

40 g/1½ oz dried cranberries

55 g/2 oz roasted cashew nuts

225 g/8 oz feta cheese, crumbled

dressing

4 tbsp extra virgin olive oil

1 tsp Dijon mustard

2 tbsp lemon juice

1 tbsp chopped fresh coriander

salt and pepper

TRADITIONAL GREEK SALAD

Make the dressing by whisking together the oil, lemon juice, garlic, sugar, and salt and pepper to taste in a small bowl. Set aside.

Cut the feta cheese into 2.5-cm/1-inch cubes. Put the lettuce, tomatoes and cucumber in a serving bowl. Scatter over the cheese and toss together.

Just before serving, whisk the dressing, pour over the salad leaves and toss together. Scatter over the olives and herbs, and serve immediately.

SERVES 4

200 g/7 oz feta cheese

½ head of iceberg lettuce or 1 lettuce, such as cos or escarole, shredded or sliced

4 tomatoes, quartered

½ cucumber, sliced

12 black olives, stoned

2 tbsp chopped fresh herbs such as oregano, flat-leaf parsley, mint or basil

dressing

6 tbsp extra virgin olive oil

2 tbsp lemon juice

1 garlic clove, crushed

pinch of sugar

salt and pepper

PANZANELLA

SERVES 4–6

250 g/9 oz stale focaccia, ciabatta or French bread

4 large vine-ripened tomatoes

about 6 tbsp extra virgin olive oil

4 red, yellow and/or orange peppers

½ cucumber

1 large red onion, finely chopped

8 canned anchovy fillets, drained and chopped

2 tbsp capers in brine, rinsed and patted dry

about 4 tbsp red wine vinegar

about 2 tbsp balsamic vinegar

salt and pepper

fresh basil leaves, to garnish

Cut the bread into 2½-cm/1-inch cubes and place in a large bowl. Working over a plate to catch any juices, quarter the tomatoes, reserving the juices. Using a teaspoon, scoop out the cores and seeds and discard, then finely chop the flesh. Add to the bread cubes. Drizzle 5 tablespoons of the oil over the mixture and toss with your hands until well coated. Pour in the reserved tomato juice and toss again. Set aside for about 30 minutes.

Preheat the barbecue. Cut the peppers in half and remove the cores and seeds. Place the peppers, skin-side down, on the grill rack and cook over medium–hot coals for 10 minutes, or until the skins are charred and the flesh is soft. Place in a polythene bag, seal and set aside for 20 minutes to allow the steam to loosen the skins. Remove and discard the skins, then finely chop the flesh. Cut the cucumber in half lengthways, then cut each half into 3 strips lengthways. Using a teaspoon, scoop out and discard the seeds. Dice the cucumber.

Add the onion, peppers, cucumber, anchovies and capers to the bread mixture and toss together. Sprinkle with the wine vinegar and balsamic vinegar and season to taste with salt and pepper. Drizzle with extra oil or vinegar if necessary, but take care that it does not become too greasy or soggy. Sprinkle the basil leaves over the salad and serve immediately.

TABBOULEH

Place the bulgar wheat in a large bowl and add enough cold water to cover. Leave to stand for 30 minutes, or until the wheat has doubled in size. Drain well and press out as much liquid as possible. Spread out the wheat on kitchen paper to dry.

Place the wheat in a serving bowl. Mix the oil and lemon juice together in a jug and season to taste with salt and pepper. Pour the lemon mixture over the wheat and leave to marinate for 1 hour.

Using a sharp knife, finely chop the spring onions, then add to the bowl with the green pepper, tomatoes, parsley and mint and toss lightly to mix. Top the salad with the olives, garnish with mint sprigs and serve immediately.

SERVES 4

175 g/6 oz bulgar wheat

3 tbsp extra virgin olive oil

4 tbsp lemon juice

4 spring onions

1 green pepper, deseeded and sliced

4 tomatoes, chopped

2 tbsp chopped fresh parsley

2 tbsp chopped fresh mint

8 black olives, stoned

salt and pepper

fresh mint sprigs, to garnish

GARLIC BREAD

SERVES 6

Preheat the barbecue. Mix together the butter, garlic and parsley in a bowl until well combined. Season with pepper to taste and mix well.

Make several lengthways cuts in the bread but be careful not to cut all the way through. Spread the flavoured butter inside the cuts and place the loaf on a large sheet of foil.

Wrap the bread in the foil, sealing the edges well to enclose completely. Cook over hot coals for 10–15 minutes, until the butter melts and the bread is piping hot. Serve immediately.

150 g/5½ oz butter, softened

3 garlic cloves, crushed

2 tbsp chopped fresh parsley

1 large or 2 small sticks of French bread

pepper

CHARGRILLED AUBERGINE BRUSCHETTA

SERVES 8

2 small aubergines

1 tbsp extra virgin olive oil, plus extra for greasing

1 large garlic clove, crushed

juice of ½ lemon, or to taste

¼ tsp cumin seeds, crushed

pinch of cayenne pepper

¼ tsp sea salt, or to taste

¼ tsp pepper, or to taste

2 tbsp chopped fresh flat-leaf parsley

1 ciabatta loaf, thickly sliced at an angle

salt

Preheat the barbecue. Prick the aubergines all over with a fork. Grease the grill rack. Cook over medium–hot coals, turning occasionally, for 15 minutes, until very charred on the outside and soft in the centre. Remove from the heat and leave until cool enough to handle.

Remove the charred skin from the aubergines and drain the flesh briefly to get rid of excess liquid. Put in a food processor with the tablespoon of oil, the garlic, lemon juice, cumin seeds, cayenne, sea salt and pepper. Whiz to a purée and tip into a serving bowl. Stir in the parsley and adjust the seasoning, adding more salt, pepper and lemon juice if necessary.

Brush the ciabatta slices on both sides with oil. Toast over medium coals for 1–2 minutes on each side, until golden. Remove from the grill. Spread a thick layer of aubergine purée over each slice, then cut in half. Serve immediately warm or at room temperature.

THREE-CHEESE DIP WITH PITTA BREAD

Preheat the barbecue. Combine the cheeses in a bowl, mixing lightly with a fork. Stir in the chives and lemon rind, and season to taste with salt and pepper.

Open out the pitta breads to make 8 halves. Slice each half crossways to make 16 pieces. Brush the cut surfaces with oil and sprinkle with a little salt and pepper.

Grease the grill rack. Grill the pitta bread over medium–hot coals, cut-side down, for 45–60 seconds on each side, or until golden. Serve immediately with the cheese dip.

SERVES 4

150 g/5½ oz cream cheese

75 g/2¾ oz feta cheese, crumbled

40 g/1½ oz Cheddar cheese, coarsely grated

3 tbsp snipped fresh chives

1 tsp coarsely grated lemon rind

4 pitta breads

olive oil, for greasing

salt and pepper

HUMMUS

Drain the chickpeas, put in a saucepan and cover with cold water. Bring to the boil, then simmer for about 2 hours, until very tender.

Drain the chickpeas, reserving a little of the liquid, and put in a food processor, reserving a few to garnish. Blend the chickpeas until smooth, gradually adding the lemon juice and enough of the reserved liquid to form a smooth, thick purée. Add the tahini paste, garlic, 3 tablespoons of the oil and the cumin and blend until smooth. Season to taste with salt and pepper.

Turn the mixture into a shallow serving dish and chill in the refrigerator for 2–3 hours before serving. To serve, mix the remaining oil with the paprika and drizzle over the top of the dish. Sprinkle with parsley and the reserved chickpeas. Serve immediately, accompanied with warm pitta bread.

SERVES 8

225 g/8 oz dried chickpeas, covered with water and soaked overnight

juice of 2 large lemons

150 ml/5 fl oz tahini paste

2 garlic cloves, crushed

4 tbsp extra virgin olive oil

small pinch of ground cumin

1 tsp paprika

1 tbsp chopped fresh flat-leaf parsley

salt and pepper

pitta bread, to serve

GRILLED PEPPER RELISH

SERVES 6–8

1 each of yellow, red and green peppers

1 tbsp extra virgin olive oil

½ tsp soft brown sugar

1 tsp balsamic vinegar

¼ tsp salt

¼ tsp paprika

Preheat the barbecue. Put the peppers onto the grill rack and cook over medium–hot coals, turning frequently, for 15 minutes, or until the skins are charred all over.

Transfer the peppers to a bowl, cover with clingfilm and leave to stand for at least 2 hours or overnight, until cold.

When the peppers are cold, hold them over a clean bowl to collect the juices and peel off the skin. Remove and discard the stem, core and seeds and finely dice the flesh.

Add the diced peppers to the juices in the bowl, then add the oil, sugar, vinegar, salt and paprika. Stir together until well mixed and serve immediately, or store in an airtight container in the refrigerator for up to 4–5 days.

SIDES & SALADS

COLESLAW

To make the dressing, mix the mayonnaise, yogurt, Tabasco
sauce and salt and pepper to taste together in a small bowl. Chill
in the refrigerator until required.

Cut the cabbage in half and then into quarters. Remove and
discard the tough centre stalk. Finely shred the cabbage leaves.
Wash the leaves under cold running water and dry thoroughly
on kitchen paper. Peel the carrots and roughly grate or shred
in a food processor or on a mandoline. Quarter and deseed the
pepper and cut the flesh into thin strips.

Mix the vegetables together in a large serving bowl and toss to
mix. Pour over the dressing and toss until the vegetables are well
coated. Cover and chill in the refrigerator until required.

SERVES 10–12

150 ml/5 fl oz mayonnaise
150 ml/5 fl oz natural yogurt
dash of Tabasco sauce
1 head of white cabbage
4 carrots
1 green pepper
salt and pepper

CUCUMBER & YOGURT DIP

Peel and coarsely grate the cucumber. Put in a sieve and squeeze out as much of the water as possible. Put the cucumber into a bowl.

Add the yogurt, garlic and mint to the cucumber and season to taste with pepper. Mix well together and chill in the refrigerator for about 2 hours before serving.

To serve, stir the cucumber and yogurt dip and transfer to a serving bowl. Garnish with mint, sprinkle with salt and pepper to taste and serve with warm pitta bread.

SERVES 4

1 small cucumber

300 ml/10 fl oz Greek yogurt

1 large garlic clove, crushed

1 tbsp chopped fresh mint or dill, plus extra to garnish

salt and pepper

warm pitta bread, to serve

GUACAMOLE

2 large ripe avocados

juice of 1 lime, or to taste

2 tsp olive oil

½ onion, finely chopped

1 fresh green chilli, such as
   poblano, deseeded and finely
   chopped

1 garlic clove, crushed

¼ tsp ground cumin

1 tbsp chopped fresh coriander,
   plus extra sprigs to garnish

salt and pepper

Cut the avocados in half lengthways and twist the halves in
opposite directions to separate. Stab the stone with the point of
a sharp knife and lift out. Peel, then roughly chop the avocado
halves and place in a non-metallic bowl. Squeeze over the lime
juice and add the oil.

   Mash the avocados with a fork to the desired consistency –
either chunky or smooth. Mix in the onion, chilli, garlic,
cumin and chopped coriander, then season to taste with salt
and pepper.

   Transfer to a serving dish and serve immediately to avoid
discoloration, garnished with coriander sprigs.

SIDES & SALADS

265

DESSERTS &
DRINKS

CHOCOLATE RUM BANANAS

Preheat the barbecue. Cut out 4 large squares of double-thickness foil and grease them with the butter.

Cut the chocolate into very small pieces. Carefully make a slit lengthways in the peel of each banana and open just wide enough to insert the chocolate. Place the chocolate pieces inside the bananas, along their lengths, then close them up.

Wrap each stuffed banana in a square of foil and cook over medium–hot coals for 5–10 minutes, or until the chocolate has melted inside the bananas.

Transfer to individual serving plates, open the foil and pour a little of the rum over each banana. Serve immediately with mascarpone cheese.

SERVES 4

1 tbsp butter

225 g/8 oz plain or milk chocolate

4 large bananas

2 tbsp rum

mascarpone cheese, to serve

NECTARINE PARCELS

Preheat the barbecue. Cut out 8 x 20-cm/8-inch squares of thick foil and grease the centre of each with butter.

Place a nectarine on each square of foil. Top each with a little of the butter, a sprinkling of sugar and a few drops of liqueur, if using. Wrap the foil into a loose parcel, sealing the edges well.

Cook over low–medium coals, covered, for 15–20 minutes, until tender. Serve warm with ice cream.

SERVES 4

8 ripe nectarines

50 g/1¾ oz unsalted butter, plus extra for greasing

3 tbsp demerara sugar

Amaretti liqueur or cognac (optional)

vanilla ice cream, to serve

CRUNCHY GINGER APPLES

SERVES 4

4 crisp, tart eating apples

2 tbsp lemon juice

2 tbsp butter, melted

2 tbsp demerara sugar

4 tbsp diced stem ginger

Preheat the barbecue. Cut the apples in half and carefully remove the seeds and cores.

Place the lemon juice, butter and sugar in 3 separate small dishes. Dip the cut side of the apples first in the lemon juice, then in the melted butter, and, finally, in the sugar.

Place the apples, cut-side down, on the grill rack and cook over medium-hot coals for 5 minutes, or until the sugar caramelizes and the apple surfaces are dark. Turn and cook for a further 5 minutes, until the skins are charred but the apples are still crunchy.

Arrange the apple halves in individual serving dishes (allowing 2 halves per serving), cut-side up, and divide the ginger among them. Serve immediately.

CHOCOLATE
FONDUE

Preheat the barbecue. To make the fondue, place the chocolate and cream in a heavy-based saucepan and gently heat over low–medium coals, stirring constantly until the chocolate has melted. Stir in the brandy until thoroughly blended and the chocolate mixture is smooth.

Thread the marshmallows onto 6 metal or wooden skewers and dip into the chocolate fondue. Serve immediately.

SERVES 6

18 marshmallows

fondue

250 g/9 oz plain chocolate, broken into pieces

150 ml/5 fl oz double cream

2 tbsp brandy

PINEAPPLE WITH MINT SUGAR

Preheat the barbecue. Peel the pineapple and slice horizontally into 2-cm/¾-inch rings. Cut the rings in half to make semi-circles and remove the core. Mix the melted butter and 2 tablespoons of the sugar in a shallow dish. Add the pineapple, turning to coat and taking care not to break the semi-circles.

Using a mortar and pestle, grind the mint with the remaining sugar and set aside.

Arrange the pineapple in a hinged wire grill basket, reserving the buttery juices. Cook for 2–3 minutes over medium–hot coals, brushing with the juices. Turn and cook for a further 2–3 minutes, brushing, until slightly charred.

Arrange in a warmed dish, sprinkle with the mint sugar and serve immediately.

SERVES 4–6

1 ripe pineapple

60 g/2¼ oz unsalted butter, melted

4 tbsp demerara sugar

2 tbsp chopped fresh mint

MIXED FRUIT KEBABS

SERVES 4

2 nectarines, halved and stoned

2 kiwi fruit

4 red plums

1 mango, peeled, halved and stoned

2 bananas, peeled and thickly sliced

8 strawberries, hulled

1 tbsp honey

3 tbsp orange liqueur

Cut the nectarine halves into wedges and place in a large shallow dish. Peel and quarter the kiwi fruit. Cut the plums in half and remove the stones. Cut the mango flesh into chunks and add to the dish with the kiwi fruit, plums, bananas and strawberries.

Mix the honey and liqueur together in a jug until well blended. Pour the mixture over the fruit and toss lightly to coat. Cover with clingfilm and leave to marinate in the refrigerator for 1 hour.

Preheat the barbecue. Drain the fruit, reserving the marinade. Thread the fruit onto several metal or pre-soaked wooden skewers and cook over medium-hot coals, turning and brushing frequently with the reserved marinade, for 5–7 minutes. Serve immediately.

PANETTONE WITH STRAWBERRIES

Hull and slice the strawberries and place them in a bowl. Add the sugar, Marsala and cinnamon. Toss the strawberries in the sugar and cinnamon mixture until they are well coated. Leave to chill in the refrigerator for at least 30 minutes.

Preheat the barbecue. When ready to serve, transfer the slices of panettone to a rack set over medium–hot coals. Cook the panettone for 1 minute on each side, or until golden brown.

Remove from the barbecue and transfer to serving plates. Top the panettone with the mascarpone cheese and the marinated strawberries. Serve immediately.

SERVES 4

225 g/8 oz strawberries

25 g/1 oz caster sugar

6 tbsp Marsala wine

½ tsp ground cinnamon

4 slices panettone

4 tbsp mascarpone cheese

CARAMELIZED APPLE RINGS

Preheat the barbecue. Remove and discard a thin slice from the top and bottom of the apples. Remove the cores and slice each apple into 3 thick rings. Put in a bowl and toss with the lemon juice to prevent discoloration.

Mix the sugar and cinnamon, and sprinkle over the apples, tossing thoroughly to coat. Brush with melted butter on both sides and place in a hinged wire grill basket, reserving any juices in the bowl.

Cook over hot coals, turning occasionally and brushing with the remaining butter and reserved juices, for 5–6 minutes, until golden and slightly charred. Serve immediately.

SERVES 4

4 crisp eating apples, such as Braeburn

juice of ½ lemon

3 tbsp demerara sugar

¼ tsp ground cinnamon

2 tbsp melted butter

TOTALLY TROPICAL PINEAPPLE

SERVES 4

1 pineapple

3 tbsp dark rum

2 tbsp muscovado sugar

1 tsp ground ginger

55 g/2 oz unsalted butter, melted

Preheat the barbecue. Using a sharp knife, cut off the crown of the pineapple, then cut the fruit into 2 cm/¾ inch thick slices. Cut away the peel from each slice and flick out the 'eyes' with the point of the knife. Stamp out the cores with an apple corer or a small pastry cutter.

Mix the rum, sugar, ginger and butter together in a jug, stirring constantly, until the sugar has dissolved. Brush the pineapple rings with the rum mixture.

Drain the pineapple, reserving the rum mixture. Cook the pineapple rings over hot coals for 3–4 minutes on each side. Transfer to serving plates and serve immediately with the reserved rum mixture poured over them.

FRUIT SKEWERS

Preheat the barbecue. Thread alternate pieces of fruit onto
4 metal or pre-soaked wooden skewers. Brush the fruit with the
maple syrup.

Put the chocolate, if using, in a heatproof bowl, set the bowl
over a saucepan of barely simmering water and heat until the
chocolate has melted.

Meanwhile, cook the skewers over medium–hot coals for
3 minutes, or until caramelized. Serve immediately drizzled with
a little of the melted chocolate, if using.

a selection of fruit, such as
   apricots, peaches, strawberries,
   mangoes, pineapple and
   bananas, prepared and cut into
   chunks

2 tbsp maple syrup

50 g/1¾ oz plain chocolate,
   melted (optional)

STUFFED FIGS

Preheat the barbecue. Cut out 8 x 18-cm/7-inch squares of foil.
Make 2 small slits in each fig, then place on a square of foil.

Put the cream cheese in a bowl. Add the cinnamon and stir
until well combined. Stuff the inside of each fig with the cream
cheese mixture, then sprinkle a teaspoon of sugar over each one.
Close the foil around each fig to make a parcel.

Place the parcels on the barbecue and cook over hot
coals, turning frequently, for about 10 minutes, or until the
figs are tender.

Transfer the figs to serving plates and serve immediately.

SERVES 4

8 fresh figs
100 g/3½ oz cream cheese
1 tsp ground cinnamon
8 tsp brown sugar

TOFFEE FRUIT KEBABS

SERVES 4

2 eating apples, cored and cut into wedges

2 firm pears, cored and cut into wedges

juice of ½ lemon

25 g/1 oz light muscovado sugar

¼ tsp ground allspice

25 g/1 oz unsalted butter, melted

toffee sauce

125 g/4½ oz butter

100 g/3½ oz light muscovado sugar

6 tbsp double cream

Preheat the barbecue. Toss the apples and pears in the lemon juice to prevent any discoloration.

Mix the sugar and allspice together and sprinkle over the fruit. Thread the fruit pieces onto 4 metal or pre-soaked wooden skewers.

To make the toffee sauce, place the butter and sugar in a saucepan and heat, stirring gently, until the butter has melted and the sugar has dissolved. Add the cream to the saucepan and bring to the boil. Boil for 1–2 minutes, then leave to cool slightly.

Meanwhile, cook the fruit kebabs over hot coals, turning and brushing frequently with the melted butter, for 5 minutes, until the fruit is just tender. Transfer the fruit kebabs to warmed serving plates and serve immediately with the cooled toffee sauce.

BANANA & CHOCOLATE S'MORES

Preheat the barbecue. Thread 2 marshmallows onto each of the 4 metal or pre-soaked wooden skewers and toast over medium–hot coals, until they soften.

Slide the marshmallows from 1 of the skewers onto a cookie, top with a square of chocolate and a few slices of banana and sandwich together with another cookie. Repeat with the remaining cookies, marshmallows, banana slices and chocolate. Serve immediately.

SERVES 4

8 marshmallows
8 chocolate chip cookies
4 squares dark chocolate
1 banana, thinly sliced

MASCARPONE PEACHES

Cut the peaches in half and remove the stones. If you are preparing this recipe in advance, press the peach halves together and wrap in clingfilm until required.

Mix the mascarpone cheese and pecans together in a bowl until well combined. Leave to chill in the refrigerator until required.

Preheat the barbecue. Brush the peach halves with the oil. Cook over medium–hot coals, turning once, for 5–10 minutes, or until tender.

Transfer the peach halves to a serving dish and top with the mascarpone mixture. Drizzle the maple syrup over the peaches and serve immediately.

SERVES 4

4 peaches

175 g/6 oz mascarpone cheese

40 g/1½ oz pecan nuts or walnuts, chopped

1 tsp sunflower oil

4 tbsp maple syrup

FRESH LEMONADE

SERVES 6

4 large lemons, preferably
   unwaxed

175 g/6 oz caster sugar

850 ml/1½ pints boiling water

ice cubes

Scrub the lemons well, then dry. Using a vegetable peeler, peel 3 of the lemons very thinly. Place the peel in a large jug or basin, add the sugar and boiling water and stir well until the sugar has dissolved. Cover the jug and leave to stand for at least 3 hours, stirring occasionally. Meanwhile, squeeze the juice from the 3 lemons and reserve.

Remove and discard the lemon peel and stir in the reserved lemon juice. Thinly slice the remaining lemon and cut the slices in half. Add to the lemonade together with the ice cubes. Stir and serve immediately.

DESSERTS & DRINKS

297

ORANGE & LIME ICED TEA

Pour the water into a saucepan and bring to the boil. Remove from the heat, add the tea bags and leave to infuse for 5 minutes. Remove the tea bags and leave the tea to cool to room temperature. Transfer to a jug, cover with clingfilm and chill in the refrigerator for at least 45 minutes.

When the tea has chilled, pour in the orange juice and lime juice. Add sugar to taste.

Take 2 glasses and rub the rims with a lime wedge, then dip them in granulated sugar to frost. Put the ice cubes into the glasses and pour over the tea. Decorate with orange or lime slices and serve immediately.

SERVES 2

300 ml/10 fl oz water

2 tea bags

100 ml/3½ fl oz orange juice

4 tbsp lime juice

1–2 tbsp brown sugar

ice cubes

to decorate

lime wedge

granulated sugar

orange or lime slices

PEACH
SMOOTHIE

Cut the peach in half, discard the stone and slice the flesh.
Reserve 1–2 slices for decoration and place the rest in a blender
or food processor.

Scoop out the seeds from the passion fruit and add to the
peach slices. If using a mandarin, peel and divide into segments
and add to the peach. With the motor running, slowly pour in the
orange juice and yogurt. Add honey to taste, if using, and blend
for 30 seconds, or until smooth.

Half fill a tumbler with crushed ice and pour over the smoothie.
Decorate with the reserved peach slices and serve immediately.

SERVES 1

1 ripe peach

1 ripe passion fruit or mandarin

2 tbsp orange juice

3 tbsp natural yogurt

1 tsp honey (optional)

crushed ice

RASPBERRY CRUSH

SERVES 4

300 g/10½ oz fresh or thawed frozen raspberries

4 tbsp orange juice

1–2 tsp honey, or to taste

crushed ice

300 ml/10 fl oz soda water

4 scoops raspberry sorbet or frozen raspberry yogurt

Reserve a few raspberries for decoration, then put the remainder in a blender or food processor. With the motor running, add the orange juice and blend for 1 minute.

Add the honey to taste and blend for 20 seconds. Half fill 4 tumblers with crushed ice, pour over the raspberry mixture and top each up with the soda water. Place a scoop of raspberry sorbet on top and serve immediately, decorated with the reserved raspberries.

SOFT SANGRIA

Put the grape juice, orange juice, cranberry juice, lemon juice, lime juice and sugar syrup into a chilled punch bowl and stir well.

Add the ice and decorate with the lemon, orange and lime slices.

SERVES 10

1.5 litres/2¾ pints red grape juice

300 ml/10 fl oz orange juice

75 ml/2½ fl oz cranberry juice

50 ml/2 fl oz lemon juice

50 ml/2 fl oz lime juice

100 ml/3½ fl oz sugar syrup

ice cubes

lemon, orange and lime slices,
   to decorate

SUMMER PUNCH

Pour the wine into a punch bowl or large glass serving bowl. Add the honey and stir well. Add the brandy, if using.

Cut any large berries into bite-sized pieces and place all the berries and mint sprigs into the wine.

Leave to stand for 15 minutes, then add the sparkling water and ice cubes. Ladle the punch into glasses or punch cups ensuring each has an ice cube and a few pieces of fruit. Serve immediately, decorated with mint sprigs.

SERVES 8

750 ml/1¼ pints rosé wine, chilled

1 tbsp honey

150 ml/5 fl oz brandy (optional)

115 g/4 oz mixed summer berries, such as raspberries, blueberries and strawberries

3–4 fresh mint sprigs, plus extra to garnish

600 ml/1 pint sparkling water, chilled

ice cubes

MARGARITA

SERVES 1

lime wedge

coarse salt

4–6 cracked ice cubes

3 measures white tequila

1 measure triple sec

2 measures lime juice

lime slice, to decorate

Rub the rim of a chilled cocktail glass with the lime wedge and then dip in a saucer of coarse salt to frost.

Put the cracked ice cubes into a cocktail shaker. Pour the tequila, triple sec and lime juice over the ice. Shake vigorously until a frost forms.

Strain into the prepared glass and decorate with the lime slice. Serve immediately.

CLUB MOJITO

Put the syrup, mint leaves and lime juice in a glass and crush or muddle the mint leaves.

Add ice and the rum, then top up with soda water to taste. Finish with a dash of Angostura bitters. Serve immediately.

1 tsp syrup de gomme

a few fresh mint leaves

juice of ½ lime

ice cubes

2 measures Jamaican rum

soda water

dash of Angostura bitters

SINGAPORE SLING

Put 4–6 of the cracked ice cubes into a cocktail shaker. Pour the gin, cherry brandy, lemon juice and grenadine over the ice. Shake vigorously until a frost forms.

Place the remaining cracked ice cubes in a chilled highball glass and strain the cocktail over them. Top up with soda water and decorate with lime peel and cocktail cherries. Serve immediately.

SERVES 1

10–12 cracked ice cubes

2 measures gin

1 measure cherry brandy

1 measure lemon juice

1 tsp grenadine

soda water

lime peel and cocktail cherries, to decorate

LONG ISLAND ICED TEA

SERVES 1

10–12 cracked ice cubes

2 measures vodka

1 measure gin

1 measure white tequila

1 measure white rum

½ measure white crème de menthe

2 measures lemon juice

1 tsp sugar syrup

cola

lime wedge, to decorate

Put 4–6 of the cracked ice cubes into a cocktail shaker. Pour the vodka, gin, tequila, rum, crème de menthe, lemon juice and sugar syrup over the ice, then shake vigorously until a frost forms.

Place the remaining cracked ice cubes in a chilled glass and strain the cocktail over them. Top up with cola and then decorate with a lime wedge. Serve immediately.

INDEX